Sun Tzu and The Art of Agile Software Delivery

Michael M. K. Cheung

Sun Tzu and The Art of Agile Software Delivery

First Edition published by ALLYSKY LIMITED 2016

ISBN-13: 978-1530335725
ISBN-10: 1530335728

Foreword

Our brains love metaphor. When I first read 'The Art of War' by Sun Tzu, I kept thinking, not about waging war, but how the ideas would apply to software development. I'm sure you've done the same kind of wondering, reading some piece of classic or philosophical literature and mapping its tenets to another area. However, I have not actually sat down and created a translation of the original work to a new domain, even though it seemed clear how I might do it! Luckily for us, Michael Cheung has taken the time and effort to do that. This will help us learn from the wisdom of Sun Tzu and, hopefully, develop better software. You might be skeptical that a text about warfare would easily map to development. Those not familiar with Sun Tzu will soon realize that his writing was not about overwhelming the enemy with powerful and/or strategic force, but was more subtle. He was all about psychological influence, long before there was any science behind this approach. Sun Tzu was also a systems thinker and we know from the increasing attention that complex adaptive systems are receiving that we all need to know more about that and its application to development. I think you're going to learn a lot: about Sun Tzu, about his philosophy, and about how apt 2500-year-old ideas can be to our present work. Enjoy!

Linda Rising Ph.D.

President and CEO of Linda Rising LLC

Co-author of Fearless Change: Patterns for Introducing New Ideas

ACKNOWLEDGEMENTS

I would like to thank Sun Tzu for his wisdom and insight and Lionel Giles for his translation of The Art of War into English in 1910.

TABLE OF CONTENTS

Introduction

In searching for the secret to how to improve Agile Software Delivery, I came across the ancient wisdom of Sun Tzu. Sun Tzu was a general who lived in northeastern China around 2,500 years ago and was a master of military tactics. Such was his genius that his military tactics and thoughts eventually were put into writing so they could be passed down to generations to come. Although the famous book, *The Art of War,* deals with situations on the battlefield and how one should apply them to a given situation, there is much wisdom in it that can be put to great use by those striving to be successful in delivering Software in an agile way.

Even though much has changed since the time of Sun Tzu, we remain subjected to key forces that existed then. The human spirit and its strengths and weaknesses are still present, and the same forces of nature and economic cycles are still with us. While the names and faces have certainly changed, the game of success is still the same as it was 2,500 years ago.

Sun Tzu and The Art of Agile Software Delivery details how the ancient warrior's codified strategies can be leveraged so anyone delivering software can benefit from his wisdom.

Success is often measured by the amount of code one has written and getting it done on time, but it is more than just that. Great software delivery is getting the right software to the user with the least amount of work done.

If you master just a fraction of Sun Tzu's wisdom you will be able to effect significant changes in the agile software development process.

I hope you enjoy reading and learning from the wisdom of Sun Tzu and wish you good luck in your future, wherever it may take you.

Michael M. K. Cheung

London

Sun Tzu and The Art of Agile Software Delivery

I. Laying Plans

Sun Tzu said: *The art of war is of vital importance to the state or nation.*

It is a matter of survival, that of life and death, a road either to safety or to ruin.

Therefore it is a subject of inquiry which can on no account be ignored.

The art of software development is of vital importance to the well-being of the business.

It is a matter of survival. In today's day and age of fast moving developments it is the businesses that can deliver great software quickly based on the demand of the market place that will survive. Those that cannot respond to change and to the needs of the market place will be left behind and ruin will shortly follow. It is critical that the push for change should not happen just in the IT department but from the CEO level where they must champion the need to be agile. Only then will the business be able to leverage the full benefit of being agile and compete in the 21st Century of software on demand.

Sun Tzu said: *The art of war has five factors that one must consider when looking at the situation that is placed in front of him in life:*

(1) The Moral Law

(2) Heaven

(3) Earth

(4) The Commander

(5) Method and Discipline

The MORAL LAW causes the people to be in agreement with their ruler so they follow him regardless of any danger they might face.

HEAVEN signifies times and seasons, day and night or hot and cold.

EARTH relates to the terrain and distances, danger and security, narrow passes or open ground, and the chances of life and death.

The COMMANDER stands for leadership that embodies attributes of wisdom, courage, kindness, and firmness.

METHOD AND DISCIPLINE relate to the chain of command and proper use of resources.

The Moral Law
Your organization is at its best and most successful when your people follow their passions and interests; your own Moral Law. Only then will different departments in your business work as one. It is the core of agile success when you are able to align the interest of business and technology on to the same roadmap.

Great agile businesses are led from the top by agile champions that provide the right environment for agility to flourish. The cultivation of autonomy, mastery and purpose are critical in developing the environment that produces business like Apple and Google.

Investing in great Agile Coaches and Scrum Masters provides the business leader the means in which to bring agreement and collaboration between business and technology.

Agile Coaches can help teams develop their mastery in their areas by the use of kaizen tools, such as holding retrospective meetings and producing retrospective action boards.

Scrum Masters help teams focus on developing their autonomy so that they are self-organizing, which allows them to become ultra-efficient in managing their efforts and intellectual capital.

Scrum Masters are also there to help teams define their purpose by creating sprint goals.

When your teams are doing the things that really motivate them, they will be waking up every morning feeling alive and buzzing with energy. When your teams are fully aligned to the business, then software delivery become very lean and better software is created rather than just working software. Most agile teams look to create working software, but why not help your teams create awesome software that really delights the customer?

Heaven

There are cycles in life and this is true for software delivery. Great agile software delivery is based on creating feedback loops. It's not just about implementing a process, but creating a living and moving system that reacts to the customer's need.

Great delivery is about having Scrum Masters and Agile Coaches help you create an environment that has feedback loops.

Examples of great feedback loops:

- Daily stand up with the Scrum Team.
- Internal playback with the Product Owner, Tester, Business Analyst once a user story is implemented within the sprint.
- Holding a retrospective meeting at the end of the

sprint.

- Demonstrating the software to the customer as early as possible

It is this feedback loop that gives the business the ability to empirically learn and create better software rather than just working software. Working software is the Scrum Team implementing the software and meeting the acceptance criteria. If you want to create great software then feedback loops will help you achieve that.

Earth

When looking to deliver that great software there is always the constraint of too little time, too little money and too many features. The ancient teachings from Sun Tzu can help in this matter. It is critical that we scan the surface of what we are trying to do. A key technique that a Scrum Master/Agile Coach would use would be to work with the product owner and help them to see what the Minimum Viable Product is - MVP. Great delivery is about doing more by doing less. The Scrum Master should guide the product owner by helping them realize what the minimum viable product is and reducing the amount of code written / effort expended. It is all about getting targeted bang for buck. I want great software without wasting the teams' efforts in doing things that won't add value to the product business value at the current moment in time. It is not just about delivering software to a deadline. It is now about delivering the right experience to the customer when it matters most. For example, the first version of the iPhone didn't support 3G; it didn't support multitasking; it didn't support 3rd party apps; you couldn't copy and paste text; you couldn't attach arbitrary files to emails; it didn't support SMS. It didn't support exchange push email; it didn't have a customizable home screen; it didn't support tethering; it hid the file system from the users; it didn't support editing office documents and it didn't support voice dialing.

But with all those missing features, it hardly mattered. The potential customers knew it, but they were looking to experience something new from Apple, which would bridge that gap between the old software paradigm and creating a rich personal user experience for the user, which we take for granted now. That is the power of having a great agile organization, which looks to deliver that great user experience at the right time. Agile teams should write less code and create a richer outcome for the business. This can only be done by empirical inspection – the teams should inspect themselves, their process, their thoughts and the customer.

A great example of doing this is the Kano Model:

The Kano Model is an insightful way of understanding and categorizing which requirements are important. All identified requirements may not be of equal importance to all customers. Kano analysis can help you rank requirements for different customers to determine which have the highest priority.

Briefly, Kano (Noriaki Kano in the 80's) stated that there are three types of customer needs or reactions to product characteristics / attributes:

- The 'Surprise & Delight' factors (Delighters). These really make your product stand out from the others. Delighters represent the unexpected – when you delight the customer by over delivering or doing something out of the ordinary. For example: for air travel it might be getting good food that actually taste good.

- The 'more is better' (Performance). For example: for Gmail it might be the amount of free storage space. Performance attribute features where there is a direct correlation between the degree of achievement and customer's satisfaction. As a consequence, businesses will tend to compete on these attributes, thus differentiating their product by spending more or less than their competitors on certain performance attributes.

- The 'must be' thing (Basic). Without this you will not sell the product. A car that does not have an engine will not sell. Basic attributes represent features that are so basic to the product that your customers just expect them to work.

It is critical to remember that today's Delighter attribute

is tomorrow's Performance attribute and in six months from now it may very well be a Basic attribute. Customer expectations continually increase, so you have to continually reiterate and reinvent your offerings.

Develop a deep understanding of the true needs of your customers, their context and their behavior. This is absolutely critical when inventing new Delighter attributes. Looking at your competitors won't help in this matter as a Delighter will not be a surprise if you are just imitating your competitors. Always look to be fresh and deliver something quick using the agile methodology.

The Commander

To implement Agile well takes courage, wisdom, kindness and firmness.

Courage: to challenge the existing structure and help the organization move from waterfall to Agile. Often people have invested their position in the waterfall methods and have things to loss. It takes courage for those people to move away from what they know to something new.

Wisdom: to know what to change at what time. Agile is not about going from 0 to 100 in ten seconds. It is about learning, growing and evolving to become better than you were yesterday. This is why kaizen activities are key to becoming more Agile. Agile is not a process, it is a mindset. It is about embracing and responding to change. It is about cultivating that at all levels in the organization.

Kindness: to gently help the people learn and change to a better version of themselves. For example, moving from a waterfall BA to an Agile BA requires that the person is kind to themselves and that they realize they may be tooled in yesterday's concepts, but as the world evolves so must they. Agile Coaches and Scrum Masters can help facilitate that transition, not just from the perspective of using Given-When-Then in their acceptance criteria, but also by helping them realize that they are more than waiters taking orders from the customer. They need to be more like doctors, helping the patient by giving them what they need and not just what they want.

Firmness is required in Agile in order to bring about change and ensure that people are following the Scrum Framework. For example, once the team have selected the user stories that will make up the sprint, then there should be a firm agreement not to add more stories into the sprint backlog until the ones that are there are completed. Firmness is required to make sure that the team are not distracted from getting on with what they have committed to for their sprint goal, rather than being side tracked by something else.

Method and Discipline

Remember the Serenity Prayer: work every day to

change the things you can change and accept those you cannot change.

Agility is something that is built over a period of time and so the people looking to implement it should be disciplined to stick to it long enough for it to take root. To implement Agile in an organization requires changing the minds of people at the CxO level, Middle Managers and those at the front lines. Only then can the organization really be fully Agile. To create agility, it is about providing the environmental container for which it can flourish.

Agile Coaches should be able to bring in big white boards that can be placed at strategic locations in the office, so that the team can be co-located to these boards.

Discipline is required by the team to follow the Scrum framework. The daily stand up should happen every day at the same time and same place. Everyone should come on time to this meeting. When people think that it is optional to come, a lack of discipline weakens the use of the meeting.

Certain great methods can be applied to ensure that people are becoming more agile. Regular use of demonstrations is one of the key ways to build agility. When the team know that something needs to be shown after it is impending then the team focuses more closely on getting working software. When internal playback is used in mid sprint, then the teams will focus more closely on getting the right software working for the sprint.

When the board is visible to the rest of the team, then everyone knows what other people are working on and it becomes a self-evidential system, which means we can see where the blockages are and where we can become leaner. Testers can see what they need to test next and developers can see what other items are in progress so that they can co-ordinate more effectively.

Don't let the board become stale. The information on the board should be updated regular throughout the day. Without this discipline the other people will start to use the board less and it won't be that useful. People won't trust the board if it is not updated. Get the team into a disciple of updating their tasks so that they are moved from 'to do', to 'in progress' and to 'done'.

Discipline: to keep running those retrospectives at the end of every sprint, because it is easy to miss one and then another one.

Discipline: to keep doing the sprint demonstration even when there is little to show. This will build the team's ability to get into a cadence when planning items for the sprint, so that they will not take on too much work and deliver nothing. It is always better to deliver a few working features that are of high quality to the business, than a load of non-working features.

Discipline: is required by the product owner to keep the

backlog groomed and well stocked with good quality user stories. They can look to have support from a business analyst and guidance from a Scrum Master.

Disciple: is required to keep those planning sessions short. In a two week sprint, planning sessions can eat into a lot of the Scrum Team's time. The team should clearly focus on what will be done and how it will be done. The key to this is getting the involvement of the PO/Business analyst to work through the stories that the team have chosen for the coming sprint. The product owner / Business analyst should be able to articulate the journey of the user stories and the acceptance criteria. These should already be captured in a tool such as JIRA or written on cards for the meeting. So the planning session should be more about clarification rather than discovery. This will keep the session short.

The team should keep the discipline of grooming their stories with the product owner each and every day rather than once every two weeks. It is much better to refine a little often, rather than trying to tackle all the stories in one session, because it takes time for understanding to grow, which is what Agile is all about. Providing the mechanism to allow change to happen and welcoming it by having regular grooming sessions enables the change to happen before the development team has written a line of code for that user story.

By following the method of Scrum, kaizen and applying good discipline, you can build a team and environment that cultivates newer levels of agility.

Sun Tzu said: *Every general should know these five components: he who knows them well can be victorious; he who is ignorant of them will fail.*

Below is a brief review of the five components you should know well in order to be successful:

The Moral Law

Take time to identify different elements in your organization and their level of agility. Bring them on board by providing Agile training so that they can know all about Agile and how it can benefit them. People only fear the things they don't know about, but if you educate them about the benefits, then they can move away from fearing Agile and become Allies and Advocates in the organization. To build a successfully agile organization, it's all about getting alignment from the different business areas. This ensures that things are flowing, rather than people looking to derail the adoption of Agile in the organization.

By getting people to think with their heads and hearts, your company's adoption of Agile at all levels will be amazing. This can be seen in organizations such as Apple and Google, which are unstoppable.

Heaven

Learn to identify where you are in the organization in its agile maturity. Different Scrum Teams will have different levels of agile maturity and so will other areas such as the business and the PMO. Looking to implement good Agile requires looking at what is happening in the organization and making changes that will help to move in synch with the organization. For example, it may be too early to look into doing automated testing or using BDD before the Business Analyst team have bought into using Gherkin Language.

It may be too early for a newly formed Scrum team to have the product owner at the retrospective until they have found their own space and confidence in where they are. Are they Forming - Storming - Norming - Performing?

A great Scrum Master / Agile Coach can evaluate these things and help the team and organization create agility at the rate that will make it agile rather than fragile.

Earth

Your Scrum Master/Agile coach should work with the teams to help them acquire the skills you need to navigate difficult times. Consider that all people involved in the Agile transformation should receive training in different aspects of Agile. The benefit of having stakeholders learn about Agile is several fold. There will be more collaboration with the rest of the team, which will mean that they will make the time for the 3 C's

- Card
- Conversation
- Confirmation

Stakeholders that have been given agile training will spend more time helping to define the card with the team.

Stakeholders who have conversations are collaborative and they help the project by creating those feedback loops, which gives us better products.

Stakeholders who provide confirmation help to ensure that things are lean because we can avoid or reduce waste by not building the wrong things. Also the chances of developing and deploying a sub optimal feature is lessened.

Teams should also look to evolve their agility because Agile is a continuous process of evolution. The Scrum Master/Agile Coach should look to increment this on a continuous basis. This is the nature of Agile.

The Commander

A good commander manages things well. A Scrum Master/Agile Coach should create points for learning by providing a clear plan for moving forward with the Agile Transformation. We should look to find ways to tackle and pay off technical debt. Teams should look to refactor often and keep thinking what process changes they can make to keep the quality high. Investing in automated testing and test driven development can be very effective in ensuring that quality is kept high and we are on a path to being able to respond to change.

All Agile projects require a certain amount of investment in the teams and tools before we can fully reach all of the benefits, but the key is to work on small but important changes. Your agile transformation should not be a big bang, but it should also not be too slow so that nothing happens. What you are looking for is similar to a virus, which slowly copies successful methods and actions to other teams and people. It changes hearts and minds on a daily basis.

Chain of Command

For Agile transformation to be effective there must be support from the CxO level of the company and also from the grass roots level. Only then can a companywide

Agile transformation programme be put on the path to success. However, the middle ground is where the most difficult changes are found. The middle manager in the organization needs to know how they will fit in when the business moves away from waterfall to Agile. Without good foundations and support from CxO level the middle manager will feel threatened by these changes. However, when they are offered training in Scrum their fears can be alleviated. It is easy to fear what we don't know, but less so once a light has been shined on the subject matter. When a CxO has the support of the middle managers in transforming the organization, then the adoption of Agile will be a lot more smoother.

Sun Tzu said: *Therefore, in your discussions, when seeking to determine the military conditions, let us compare and contrast the issues.*

Which of the two rulers has the Moral law?

The two rulers are the head and heart. Do you follow your head or your heart, or both? If your head and heart are in agreement, chances are good you're heading in the right direction.

How many times have you been held back when your mind was focused on attaining a certain goal, but your heart was not?

Jason, an average developer, is given a spec and a component to write and has worked in component teams. He writes his code for the new component and passes it on to the next team. He works in a waterfall organization and never sees what the component is used for or what the product is.

Richard, on the other hand, works in an Agile team and works with the product owner and testers to build software, which is viewed by the product owner once the user story has been implemented. Richard is always excited about getting his user story ready for internal playback to the product owner in the next few days. He feels pretty motivated because he is able to show all the cool new features that he has implemented in the last few days. He is given a lot of autonomy by the Scrum Master / Product owner when he is working on the user story. Once the playback of the user story is done Richard feels a sense of great pride and purpose as he can see that his hard efforts are going to help the company in selling this product and that the customers are really going to love it.

How many times has your software development team been held back when their heart was focused on attaining a certain goal but the other part of the business was not there? If a product owner / stakeholder doesn't have time to watch the internal playback because they are too busy then they need to be changed or helped to see the wisdom of doing what is best for the project and team.

A passionate product owner can work wonders for the productivity of the team. An absent product owner or one that has very little time for demos is one that will slow the team down and eventually the team will become demotivated. They will stop producing high quality work as the product owner cannot be bothered to view the software, so why should the Scrum team care?

Of the two rulers, which has the most capability?

Which is your strongest asset; your head or your heart?

Some people are very analytical and logical. Other people work from the heart.

If you are analytical and logical, you may want to focus on the automation part of making the team Agile. You should focus on TDD, BDD, continuous integration and automation. You team will benefit from these and so will the project.

Passionate teams can also focus on the collaboration part and creative aspects, such as welcoming change and story mapping for better understanding of the user story journey and building the backlog.

It is the marriage of the two, however, where your teams will really start to progress. If your team can embrace collaboration, story mapping, retrospectives, estimations, pair programming, TDD, BDD, Automation and CI then they will be extremely Agile.

Given Heaven and Earth, where are the advantages to be found?

Given the current environment in which you are developing software, would it make sense for you to start with the logical aspect first or the people part first?

As most agile adoptions are not done in a vacuum, it is common for a team to start by bringing in a Scrum Master who will help the team by working with someone from business and getting the right person onboard as a product owner. Select the right product owner and good things can follow – select the wrong one and it will be an uphill battle. Once you have selected a great product owner, you need to start by thinking about where the team sits. Are they in a space where collaboration can happen? This may seem like common sense, but often teams are in non-agile office spaces and the CxO wants them to be agile, but is not aligned with providing the right space for that to happen.

You can't grow kiwis in a desert, so don't expect to grow agile teams in non-agile spaces.

So it is key to create an agile space for the team to

flourish. This involves bringing in whiteboards and creating plenty of writing space. The team should have easy access to the whiteboards, so they can update them often on a daily basis when the status changes.

When these things are in place and teams can feel free to talk without feeling and they are disturbing those around them, then we have the basic core of an agile environment in place.

The Scrum Framework should then be put into place and once these aspects have been met then advance logical topics, such as TDD, BDD, CI etc. can be addressed.

Of the two sides, on which has the most rigorous discipline been applied?

Whether you are a logical thinker or of the heart, when pursuing any Agile Transformation you should be disciplined in your approach. Focus your efforts to the best of your abilities. Commit to achieving a high level of success. Stay disciplined and keep moving forward.

Which of the armed forces are stronger?

Always know your team's strongest skills and work to

make sure that you build T-shaped Scrum members rather than I-shaped Scrum members. T-shaped members will be cross functional and able to have their specialist areas, but can also help with other areas. Whereas, I-shaped Scrum Members who only have a specialism will slow the team's overall velocity down. This is because a Scrum Team is usually small and nimble so each member really makes a difference to the team's ability to get work done.

On what side are captains and foot soldiers more highly trained?

To know your team strengths and weaknesses you need to inspect and adapt often. The best way to do this is to run retrospectives.

In your retrospective you can spend time building a team radar, which will help you determine your team's strengths and weaknesses.

To do this you can present the 12 agile principles to the team and then ask them to score on a scale of 0 to 10 for each of the agile principles.

0 being the lowest and 10 being the highest

The Scrum Master can then help the team work on and update their team radar every two weeks. You should be able to help the team find different activities/tasks which they can take on to build their agility.

In which military is there the greater reliability for both reward and punishment?

In which areas have your team excelled and in which areas have they failed?

Change habits that in the past have led to less-than-optimal results. Avoid doing the same actions over and over simply because your team are set in their routine. You team will never see improved results until you identify and pursue what's most effective.

Get your team to do something in a different way to see new change. Consider asking them to find a new angle or learn a new set of skills. It is useful to ask developers to review test script written by testers and ask developers to see things from the tester's perspective.

Even writing code in a different way can help them see things in a new and improved way.

Once you've identified what works well, stick with it and focus on improving it through implementation and generating great results.

Sun Tzu said: *Given these seven concerns one can forecast victory or defeat.*

The more inspection and adaption your team does, the better their chances are of implementing good Agile. Keep in mind that your team should keep on refining their approach to being agile through numerous feedback loops, which operate at different sizes.

In working on an agile project we do not have to discard our old tool, but we can re-tool and use them anew.

To help us with forecasting our victory in delivering the project well and on time we need to use good project management tools.

We can still do SWOT analysis (strengths, weaknesses, opportunities, and threats), pros and cons lists, business plans, and cost-benefit analysis.

SWOT analysis identifies the objective of a project as well as the internal and external factors that help or hinder the achievement of that objective.

The following line items are considered via SWOT analysis:

Strengths: characteristics that put a project at an

advantage.

Weaknesses: characteristics that put a project at a disadvantage

Opportunities: opportunities available to a project

Threats: external factors that threaten the success of a project.

Maintaining a list of these in the team area will help them focus on the project. You can also look to build a project issue Kanban board which can be useful for ensuring that project issues are being made visible and handled.

Pros and Cons Lists can provide a good view of ideal and less-than-ideal courses of action. Consider, for example, possible pros and cons of what the social media Mobile Phone App will do for the customer:

Pros

- It will make me look cool
- It will make me stand out more
- It will help me fit in at college
- It will help me express something I like
- It will help me express my sense of style
- It might help me meet new and exciting people.

Cons

- It might make me feel exposed
- It will be difficult for me to remove my digital foot print
- It might make me a target for scammers
- It may hinder my ability to get a job

Project Plans are designed to focus the team on all the tasks and the order in which they need to be done in. Being Agile does not mean we discard the project plan. It means we need to be agile about what work we are going to do so that we meet the project plan.

In your project plan there will be a fixed number of sprints, which you are given in order to get the work done. Being agile will mean we can build a plan of what backlog items will fill the sprints, but along the way you might find that you need to drop some of the backlog items out of scope so that you can focus on other backlog items, which are now more important. As your team progress through the project they and the product owner will learn more about what is kept in order to make the project a success and your plan needs to be Agile enough to incorporate those elements.

Disciplined Agile Delivery is a good place to start if your organization has been used to working on projects that were waterfall / Prince 2 driven. You will be able to add elements in that will help you get things delivered.

You should look to build a vision document that describes a compelling idea or values or state for a particular product or service. It defines the stakeholder's view of the product/service to be developed, specifically in terms of stakeholder's key needs and features.

You should also look to build a technical strategy document, which outlines at high level the Technology, Business architecture and User Interface UI. Will you be configuring an existing COTs, building a new COTs or building from scratch?

You should also look to build an initial release plan. Key things are to build a product backlog and provide high level estimates on the backlog items. So you can determine the number of sprints that you will need and the size and composition of the teams. This will help to make sure that your team is on track with project time lines.

Cost-benefit analysis provides a systematic process for calculating and comparing likely benefits and costs of a project.

One of the key things you should do is to order your product backlog. There are different ways to do this. You could do it in order of priority to the business, you could do it based on technical consideration i.e. login screen first, modeling, saving, edit etc.

You can look to create a calculated metric which is used to score the value of each feature. This calculated metric could then use cost benefit analysis to help with this ordering.

Scrum Dev Team A: Has 3 developers and 1 tester

3 developers cost 3*$500 per day = $1500

1 tester cost 1*$400 per day = $400

Total cost of Scrum Team per day is $1900

If a team has a velocity of 20 story points per 2 week sprint, then 20/10 day = 2 story points per day.

So the cost of doing, for example. feature A: Which is estimated to take 10 points will be:

10 points / 2 story points per day = 5 days' worth of work.

5*$1900 = $9,500

Feature A Cost $9500

If feature A gets in the product in the first release cycle and brings in 1000 new customers, which subscribe to the service at $50 a year:

Sales Generated is $50 * 1000 = $50,000

So return is $50,000/$9,500 = 5.26

Compare this to feature B:

Feature B has been sized to be 20 story points

Which will cost:

20 pts / 2 = 10 days' worth of work

10 * $1900 = $19,000

Feature B will cost $19,000

Now, what is the benefit of this feature to the market if it gets release in the current release cycle?

If feature B get in the product in the first release cycle and brings in 300 new customers who subscribe to the service at $50 a year:

Sales Generated is $50 * 300 = $15,000

So return is $15,000/$19,500 = 0.77

A higher number is better i.e. Sales Generated / Cost to develop feature => we want more sales and lower cost to develop.

We can see that Feature A has a score of 5.26, which gives us more bang for buck vs Feature B which has a score of 0.77. A score of less than 1 is effectively going to be losing money as it returned less than it cost to make.

So when ordering the backlog:

Feature A is ordered above Feature B

As you do this for all the product backlog items you should be able to see clearly which features are going to be giving the most business value.

This analysis results in having a product backlog, which tell us how much it will cost to develop the backlog and which features are the most valuable.

MoSCoW Method

Moscow method is a prioritization technique used in management, business analysis and project management.

The letters stand for:

- Must Have
- Should Have
- Could Have
- Won't Have this time

Must have:

It is important to define what 'must have' means, because they will inform us of the minimum usable subset of features which the project guarantees to deliver.

'Must have' consideration for its definition may include:

- Key part of user experience for this release
- Not legal without it
- Unsafe without it

Should have:

- Important but not essential
- Maybe not the best user experience without it but the product will still meet its product use without it
- A workaround exists if we don't implement this feature

Could have:

- People would like it but it is not so important
- Less impact if left out compared to the 'should have'

Won't have:

These are features that the project team has agreed it will not deliver this time. They are recorded in the product backlog as 'won't have', which will help to clarify the scope of the project and thus avoid the re-introduction via the backdoor route at a later date in the current release. This is key because it will help manage the expectation of some of the requirements i.e. the ones marked as 'won't have' will simply not get in the current release.

Product Backlog Items – PBI

Having good product backlog items can make all the difference in delivering the project on time.

You should consider a few key things for your product backlog items:

- Consider using the user story format
- Have a definition of sprint ready, i.e. when do you consider a user story good enough to take into a sprint?
- Follow the INVEST mnemonic.

  The user story format is a great way to represent your customer needs.

  It should follow the format:

  As a <Type of User>, I want <some goal> so that <some reason>

  By putting yourself in the first person perspective the product owner will have a better understanding of what the feature should be doing.

A lot of time can be wasted in planning sessions where the User Story is not sprint ready. Rather than the planning session being about planning it can become all about defining the requirements.

Ideally, the team should come up with a definition of a user story item being sprint ready.

For example:

Sprint Ready User Stories are sized where the estimate is no more than a sprint worth of work. Follow the INVEST format and have Gherkin Syntax for the acceptance criteria.

Following the INVEST format will help ensure that your stories are well formed.

- Independent stories are easier to plan and deliver vs dependent stories. So try to break them up if possible.
- Negotiable - stories should be open to being changed and rewritten until they are part of an iteration
- Valuable - a story should delivery value to the user
- Estimable - a story should always be sized before going into a sprint
- Small - a story should be broken-down until it

can be done in a sprint.

- Testable – a story should be one that can make test development possible.

Grooming the backlog

Agile is all about welcoming change and that means your team should be looking to groom the backlog, often at least one a sprint for two hours. But, a little each and every day will work better. You should groom product backlog items that are going to be in the next sprint two weeks before you enter them into the sprint because it will take a few sessions to ensure they are Sprint Ready.

Velocity

Know your team's velocity. Know your product backlog. 100 projects – 100 victories. Well, that's what we would like to achieve and the secret is knowing as much as possible and making decision at the latest possible moment. Defer decisions until the last possible chance so you have all the information at hand to make key decision.

Sun Tzu said: *The general that listens to my advice and acts upon it will conquer. The general that does not listen to my advice or act upon it will suffer a great defeat.*

Taking steps to conduct analysis, but then disregarding its results will end in failure.

Tom's team told him that they had a velocity of 25 story points and having sized the product backlog, Tom found that the total size was 300 points. Tom decided that the team could probably go faster and do 50 story points.

Tom calculated that 300 / 50 = 6 sprints was what he needed.

Tom built his project plan around this instead of 300 / 25 = 12 sprints.

The team were able to deliver the project in 9 sprints, which was better than the 12 sprints. Tom's analysis lead him to delivering the work 3 sprints behind his 6 sprint estimate. Had tom listen to his team, he could have given a range of between 6 and 12 or taken an average and put it closer to 9 sprints.

The people who know the work best are the ones who are doing it. One would do well to listen to all estimates and build a plan around all available information.

Had Tom listened to the team prior to building his project plan on his own estimates, he may have been successful. Unfortunately, Tom didn't listen to his team and acted upon the findings of his own analysis.

Listen to your research and act accordingly.

Sun Tzu said: *While listening to my advice, be ready to follow any helpful circumstances over and beyond that of the ordinary rules.*

Sometimes special situations occur and you may need to go beyond the ordinary rules:

- Dropping a user story from a sprint when it became apparent that it is not needed.
- Aligning an extra developer/tester from another team to your scrum team for a sprint or two.
- Working extra time on a critical release

Sun Tzu Said: *When circumstances are favorable, one should adapt one's plans to keep up with the new improved situation.*

Agile adoption is something that works much like a spreading virus.

You cannot rush in and ask everyone to be Agile in a day. To be successful you need to build upon the adoption on a daily basis and there will be good days and bad days to try out new things. Always look to find the good day to offer a new challenge or change to the environment. Demonstrate the success in a small way first and then show others what you did to make it work better. This will help the organization to adopt Agile, rather than it being a carpet bombing operation of sudden change. You need to win people over, one Agile initiative at a time.

Sun Tzu Said: *All conflicts are based on deception.*

Conflicts are based on deception and what we need to do in the Agile environment is to keep all information transparent. Transparency is one of the best way to create agility because the shared understanding and cooperation that transparency creates reduces conflict and enhances productivity.

Sun Tzu Said: *When the enemy is secure at all points, be prepared for him. If he is of superior strength, evade him.*

When there are people who are blockers to adopting Agile then the best way to win them over is to not tackle their dis-engagement or lack of interest. But to start using Agile where it can be seeded and then help them see the benefits through the power of helping them to see that this is a better way of working. Seeing is believing. List down all of their objections and find any areas in the organization where you can show that it does work for these objections.

Sun Tzu Said: *If your enemy is trying to rest then keep him unsettled.*

It is easy to fall into bad habits of going back into the waterfall way of doing things, so it is key to keep all parties in the Agile Adoption engaged with new and exciting aspects.

Try different retrospective format – look to build new information radiators and ensure that grooming sessions happen frequently. Most of all, keep the product owner involved in the sprint demonstration.

You could even think about asking them to be interactive in the sprint demo.

Sun Tzu Said: *If your enemy forces are cohesive, break them apart.*

Delivering software is all about taking a big problem and breaking it down in smaller and more manageable chunks.

Often we will have a big user story, which is called an epic and is too big to take into a sprint. The best option is to look at breaking the epic down into smaller user stories that can be shared among the Scrum Team.

An epic could be 100 story points and the user stories that are sprintable should be 13 point or less.

There are many ways to break an epic down, but the key thing to remember is to do so in a way that delivers single user stories, which provides a thin slice of functionality that is end to end, rather than horizontally.

There are a number of strategies for splitting user stories:

Strategy 1: Split by workflow steps

If user stories involve a workflow of some kind, the item can usually be broken up into individual steps:

Step 1: Login

Step 2: Search

Step 3: View

Step 4: Add to cart

Step 5: Checkout

Step 6: Payment

Step 7: Generate Invoice and Shipping details.

Strategy 2: Split by business rules

As a customer of a bank, I want to pay my bill so that I can settle my account.

As a customer **I want to** pay by cash **So that** I can settle my account

As a customer **I want to** pay by cheque **So that** I can settle my account

Strategy 3: Split by happy / unhappy flow

As a customer of a bank **I want to** pay my wedding organizer **So that** I can have a great wedding

As a customer of a bank **I want** to stop my cheque **so that** I don't pay my builder

Strategy 4: Split by input options

As a customer of a bank **I want to** be able to pay money in by ATM **so that** I can increase my account balance

As a customer of a bank **I want to** be able to pay money in by Internet Transfer **so that** I can increase my account balance

Strategy 5: Split by datatypes or parameters

Some user stories can be split by the datatypes they return or the parameters they handle.

As a Bank Customer **I want to** search by Payment No **So that** I can find my payment quickly

As a Bank Customer **I want to** search by Payment Amount **So that** I can find my payment quickly

Strategy 6: Split by operations

User stories can be involved in a number of operations such as the CRUD ones.

- Create
- Read
- Update
- Delete

As a Bank Manager I want to Manage my customer details

This can be broken down into:

As a Bank Manager I want to Create my customer details.

As a Bank Manager I want to Read my customer details.

As a Bank Manager I want to Update my customer details.

As a Bank Manager I want to Delete my customer details.

Strategy 7: Split by roles

User stories can often involve a number of roles, which may perform a number of functions, such as the one below:

As a Bank Employee **I want to** manage my customer details

As a Bank Clerk **I want to** Read my customer Details

As a Bank Supervisor **I want to** Update my customer Details

As a Bank Manager **I want to** Delete my customer Details

Sun Tzu Said: *When your enemy does not expect you, you must launch your attack and thus catch him of guard.*

Agile is not just about moving software to the door faster! It's not about moving bad UI experience software to the market faster. It's also about getting the right UI software out of the door faster! It is important to look at the competitors in your sector and focus on bringing the right features to market as early as possible – thus catching him off guard. This can only be done by being able to have good feedback loops with your audience – internal and external and making rapid changes to meet those needs. This is one of the key things an Agile organization should be doing to get in alignment with the market place.

Sun Tzu Said: *Military strategies which give you the edge and thus lead you to victory must remain secret in order for them to be effective.*

When developing innovative approaches to getting

better software out there, you should always look to retain your best developers, testers and don't forget to keep your great Scrum Master/Agile Coaches. They are the glue that help keep the cogs of the machine running smoothly. The best companies always look to keep their best people by creating an innovative, challenging and fun environment to work in. Agile is about doing this and still making sure you get business value to boot.

Sun Tzu said: *Before a battle is fought, the wise general must consider all the issues that are presented in the battlefield.*

The unwise general who loses his battle has considered only a few of the important issues before he launches his attack.

He who analyzes more issues will be gifted with victory.

He who considers but a few will have defeat handed to him.

One can foresee who is likely to win or lose given how they prepare for battle. A general who does no analysis of the issues will be defeated as likely as night follows day.

Agile is not about developing the software without planning. It's about continually understanding where the delivery is going on a daily basis by making all available information transparent to all team members and reacting to risk and issues early. In regular waterfall you plan in the beginning and then try to resist any thing that would look to change that plan via the dreaded change request. In Agile we welcome that change by creating the environment where we are re-planning on a daily basis or as and when needed. Item in the product backlog can and should adjust to the latest information while we are delivering the project, without changing the deadline.

II. Waging War

Sun Tzu said: *In the theatre of war, there are thousands of cavalry and mail-clad soldiers which have enough provisions to carry them many miles. The cost on the front line and at home will reach the total of thousands of ounces of silver per day. Such is the cost of running an army of 100,000 soldiers.*

Be sure up front that you've accumulated enough resources to complete a task before you undertake it.

In an Agile project you should ensure that you have a team that is stable. Look to have a good cross functional team, which has a size of at least 3 to 9 people in the Scrum development team.

For a team of 9 you could have 6 developers and 3 testers.

For a team of 3 you could have 2 developers and 1 tester.

It is also important to see if you can have a dedicated business analyst working with your product owner to help ensure that a good consistent flow of user stories get written.

A product owner may be the owner of the user stories, but a business analyst will ensure that they are being created quickly enough, so that the pipeline does not slow down when some heavy lifting is required.

Having a stable team and a great product owner and BA will help to keep things moving smoothly, but you should also ensure that you have enough time to build the MVP.

The MVP is the minimum viable product, which is essential to getting your first release done.

To ensure that you have planned for your MVP you should have sized all product items that make up the MVP so that you know how many story points it will take to complete the MVP.

For example the MVP might end up being 500 story points.

If your team can complete around 25 story points per sprint then you have 500/25 = 20 sprints worth of work.

If your sprints are 2 week iteration then you have about 40 weeks' worth of work.

You might need to consider the focus factor in your calculations, for example in a given day your team might have only 75% of their time free for doing development work.

So your velocity may be 25*0.75 =18.75

Base on this 500/18.75 = 26.67 sprints worth of work.

If your sprints are 2 week iteration then you have about 54 weeks' worth of work.

So your projected range might be between 40 weeks and 54 weeks.

You should plan accordingly, as Agile is not a magic silver bullet in software delivery. You still need to factor in some buffer so that your team can accommodate change that Agile creates, otherwise people will feel it is fragile rather than Agile.

If you set the timeline on the 40 week side then you won't have built in any ability to handle change, which Agile will throw up - you can be sure that will happen.

The other way is to build your product backlog so that you have Must have, Should have, Could have in the backlog, so you have the ability to de-scope user stories if you should find yourself running behind.

In Agile - It is time and cost that are fixed and scope is the variability in the iron triangle equation.

He who builds his triangle with fixed time, fixed cost and fixed scope will surely fail.

Sun Tzu said: *When you engage in actual fighting, if victory is long in coming, you will exhaust all your resources and the resources of the Nation will not be equal to the strain brought onto it.*

Starting any project or taking on any task can result in a protracted experience. Prepare for the fact your various types of resources may be strained and surround yourself with those who are willing and able to help.

If you are starting a large scale project that will take at least a year or two to complete then make sure you have arranged things so that there is a sustainable pace. You can't have your developers working every weekend or late every day. Make sure that you have been conservative in your estimates because you should welcome change and to do that you need to create the space in your project plan so that change can happen. You want to encourage change because that is a good sign that your customers are getting what they want, as seldom do we get everything right in the beginning. No matter how hard we try to analyze the requirement, we won't and can't know everything up front. Rather than blocking change, ensure you can embrace it by building in space to accommodate it. You may also look to reprioritize what is needed by de-scoping items that are less important to the current release.

Sun Tzu Said: *When you have battled long and hard and your supplies are exhausted and your weapons are of no use, you will find other factions will rise up and take up arms against you. Then no matter how wise or able, you will not be able to prevent your own demise.*

When you're in a protracted situation in which your resources have become exhausted your enemies will try to strike you down.

If you work you scrum development team into exhaustion then you will find that illness and high turnover is your enemy. Your best developers will start to leave your team and the others will get sick. Maybe your competitors will lure your best people away. To prevent this, ensure that you work at a sustainable pace and keep your team refreshed by looking to make sure that everyone is enjoying their work and are highly motivated.

Look to use Dan Pink's motivational concept - MAP

Motivation is:

- Mastery
- Autonomy
- Purpose

Let people have targets to master their areas in the project. Help them become autonomous in their work as a self-organizing team. Help them find their purpose by doing regular retrospective and sprint demos.

Your team wants to know how they have been helping to build a better product and that means involving them with the product development team, so that they know what they are building and who they are doing it for.

Building personas at the start of the project can be very useful in helping your team understand the customer base. The product owner or business analyst should assist in this matter - it should be a collective thing for the whole team.

Sun Tzu said: *In war only fools rush in but equally delays have never been associated with being clever either.*

Everyone one wants to start coding as quickly as possible, but it is equally important to remember to do things in a way that ensures the project will be developing a solid foundation over its lifetime rather than incurring technical debt. Try not to build a website of platform that is held together by hacks and hard coded magic numbers. Using design patterns when useful can help in this matter, but don't go the other way and over engineer with too many design patterns, just for the sake of using them.

Things to remember

- Do some up front thinking for your technical strategy. You should evolve your design, but this also means you should have a basic initial technical strategy to start with.
- Think about leveraging existing enterprise assets. You should think about what libraries, patterns, templates and guideline you can reuse.
- Your team should have an architecture owner that can guide the team, so that the developer can be guided in their technical decisions.
- Your team should think about what can be refactored in the code base so that it is always kept in good condition.
- Regression test on a regular basis to ensure that you can detect defect and resolve them quickly
- Automate code / analysis – CI Tools and Build Tool are key to ensuring you are tackling technical debt.
- Measure technical debt – it is always important to look for ways to keep a check on this. Consider inspecting code often.
- Reducing technical debt should be part of the culture of your agile team. Rushing in to write code without thinking about the best way to do it will create issues later on.

Sun Tzu said: *No country has benefited from having a protracted campaign in the arena of warfare.*

Do not spend all your time at war with those around you. You can be right but you don't have to impose your ideas on others all the time. Don't waste your energy and resources trying to convince others that your way is the correct way.

To build a great Agile team you should avoid wasting energy on getting into conflicts. Instead, you should save your resources and put them to use in developing and improving your team, process, product and service.

Don't try to beat the whole organization into using Agile in one go. Focus on winning small battles on a regular basis but accept when you have make a poor call and be willing to adjust your strategies to take on a new challenge.

Sun Tzu said: *When one has made themselves conversant with the evils of war only then can one know all the most profitable ways to gain from it.*

Sometimes the only way that an Agile team can grow is at the expense of the existing structure. Teams that have become stale may need to be restructured so that new life can be brought into them. A team that is anti-agile may need to be disbanded so that they can be recast again in the fires or Agile so that they will be renewed.

This rebuilding of the team will give all new members the chance to speak their minds and for them to try new things. If a new member joins an established team that has old values then they will seek to take the new member and make them work in the old way.

By creating a new agile team it is a lot easier to start afresh with new impetus.

Sun Tzu said: *The skilled general does not need to construct an extra set of defenses or double his supplies.*

Consider what I call the 'max-min principle': It is just as important to maximize the benefit as it is to minimize costs associated with that benefit. This is also known as the 'min-max principle'. Reduce costs expended—whether in the form of time, money, physical effort, or mental effort—while working to maximize the results and benefits of the task at hand.

Lean thinking is key to helping the team work with the min-max principle.

1. Eliminate waste:

   Your team should look to avoid writing unnecessary code or functionality.

   Stop starting more work than can be completed.

   Task switching.

2. Build Quality In:

   Your team can look to address this by using Test Driven development and Pair Programming.

3. Create Knowledge:

   Often there will be a project plan created at the start of the project and this will be the road map for going forward, but will it be enough to drive the project to success? What is needed in an Agile project is the creation of knowledge. There should be a lot of visual boards, which tell us on a daily basis where things are and what people are working on. This helps us to create knowledge and drive an agile project forward. It's so simple yet misunderstood that BIG visual boards are critical to getting an agile project off the ground. Stop using them to keep stale information - use them to build a living document of what is going on in the project and get everyone around them on a daily basis. No ifs or buts.

   Also remember that it is useful to have a wiki to allow the teams to share information across different physical locations.

4. Defer Commitment:

   You should look to defer commitment to the last possible moment, so that you have as much up to date information as possible to make a good decision on.

   Sprint planning helps to make sure that you defer commitment by ensuring that what is going to be built and how it should be built is done as late as possible, so we can learn from our previous sprints.

5. Deliver fast:

   Keep things moving by removing blockers as soon as they occur. Have a visual whiteboard which tracks your team's sprint effort and make some stop sign which can be used to highlight items that are blocked. Every day an item is block is a delay that can have a knock on effect to the rest of the project and the wider programme.

   Try not to over engineer solutions by using BUF - Big Up Front design. Instead, let the design evolve out of the development at hand.

   Build a simple solution and get it to market and then get feedback and iterate.

   Create those blue post it notes which show that this task is dependent on another team. Use colorful post-it notes to help define key areas of focus on your scrum board.

   Agile teams need to collaborate often to ensure that we are not waiting for dev or test or the product owner to pass on critical information which is slowing things down. Remember to K.I.S.S when trying to get things done.

6. Respect People

Treat everyone with the same respect that you expect people to treat you with. Motivated individuals are much better for the project than those who are hire guns. What you want is people enjoying the work that they are doing and feeling valued.

Letting everyone have their say is a healthy thing, which should keep everyone on a good path.

7. Optimize the Whole:

   It important to remember that optimizing the team is useful and will add value, but you should also look at the whole value stream and work on that too.

   There is time spent by the product owner, stakeholders and development and testing that can be optimized increases efficiency. We should look to map the time spent in different areas and look to see how we can make the pipeline run smoothly.

Sun Tzu said: *When you go to war you should bring resources with you but always look to forage on the enemy.*

When looking to adopt agile in a new environment it is important to bring new ideas to the team, but the best place to start is to run a retrospective to see where the team currently are on a number of key areas. You should find out what their level of maturity is with welcoming change, test driven development, automation, estimations etc. Once you have gathered this data then you can start to adapt. Agile is an empirical process and that means inspecting and adapting. It's not about 'one size fits all' and trying to force a certain solution to each and every team or organization.

Sun Tzu said: *If your state treasury is suffering from poverty then your army will be underfunded and your people impoverished.*

If you are looking to adopt Agile without spending a certain amount of money to make it work, then you will not have a successful adoption.

The basic minimum should be clear:

- Lot of writable space - Really big whiteboards
- Decent stationary - Quality post-it notes and whiteboard pens are a must
- A decent coffee/tea facility
- High spec machines with dual monitors
- Desk space to allow pair programming
- Training budget to encourage teams to grow
- Software budget for books and CI Tools

It is very difficult or near impossible to do good Agile without the above being addressed. People trying to implement Agile tend to try to do it without the above things in place. It is more than having a daily meeting and following the processes because it won't work fully without the correct tools and environment. It so simple but people do tend to overlook these things.

Sun Tzu said: *An army that is far away will require much resources from its homeland.*

When your team is far away from the Scrumboard / Kanban Board they will find it difficult to update it on a regular basis. Good Agile implementation makes sure the board is right next to the scrum team and that it is updated regularly. You want the most up to date information possible at hand - fresh from the people actually doing the work.

If you are working with non-collocated teams then make sure you use a good Agile tool like JIRA to ensure the team have an updated view of the Electronic Scrum board. It's good to ask the team to update the electronic board after the daily stand up.

Sun Tzu said: *When the homeland has it resources drained to support a faraway army then famine will ensue and so will a drop in maintenance of public services.*

When your team run into more obstacles than anticipated and their morale is running low they may begin to feel apathetic. Depression may even set in. Guard against this happening and do what you can to prevent it via healthy habits related to their diet, sleep, and exercise. Also be sure to ask for help when you need it.

If your team has waged a long campaign that has not been especially successful then staff morale may become low and the team energy may suffer. Find ways to turn this around as quickly as possible.

When your team are exhausted and drained mentally and physically, they are more likely to make bad judgment calls. Such mistakes can be very expensive.

When the environment or project is giving you a beating don't keep on going at it. Take a break to reassess your strategy, returning only after you've had time to recuperate and prepare a new plan of attack – remember to run retrospective and have action points to take away.

Sun Tzu said: *When the resources have been stripped from the homeland the people will suffer even more and will have a third of their money taken by the government so they can pay for someone to fix the broken chariots and buy new horses and swords and bows. Adding in for replacement of supplies you can consider that 40 percent of the homeland income will be diverted to the government treasury for the paying of all these costs.*

If your team works to a point at which you're trying to do too many things and getting run down then they will start to become burnt out and less efficient.

The cost of replacing staff in your business can also be very expensive. Take steps to keep morale high in your office so your business doesn't have to experience such costly disruptions.

Building your Agile team takes time, but can be lost in a blink of an eye due a few bad decisions. Guard against this happening by taking time to rest and reassess your teams and project strategy.

Sun Tzu said: *A wise general who understands these matters will forage on the enemy instead of taking from his homeland.*

He will consider that one cart of the enemy's provisions is worth as much as 10 times his own. He need not drain his own supplies and put strain on his countrymen when he can devastate his enemy by taking from them.

Look for and take advantage of lessons learnt from other Agile teams by seeking out and looking at what worked well in other teams and organizations.

Always look to find a way to conserve your efforts so that you can start a new project with the original members intact.

Sun Tzu said: *In warfare you must be able to cajole your men into battle by letting them know of the rewards they will gain when the enemy is defeated. Promise spoils of war to your men who fight with heart. Then capture and use whatever resources you find on the battlefield, be it equipment or men, to substantially improve your own resources as well as your soldiers' morale, loyalty, and resolve.*

Take care of those who helped you succeed. Make sure they know they are appreciated and share with them the many tangible rewards of your success.

Sun Tzu said: *In battle one should strive for a short campaign and a great victory.*

In any project or campaign the objective is to reach your goal by utilizing the least amount of resources.

SMART is a mnemonic to help set such important objectives:
Specific – make it well defined

Measurable - know when it is achieved (i.e. define the finish line)
Achievable - identify other examples
Realistic - consider your resources, such as money, time, and knowledge
Time-bound - set a timeframe for the project (e.g. one year)

The SMART criteria can be used as a framework before the start of any new project. When learning to drive, for example, one of your objectives may be to get a driver's license as quickly as possible.

Specific goal = Get driver's license

Measurable result = Examiner gives me a license

Achievability proof = My friends and family members have driver's licenses

Realistic plan, including resources = I can invest two days per week in learning to drive, read books from the library or documents online about driving, and use some of the $2K my parents are paying toward my driving lessons. Since $20 a lesson x 40 hrs = $800 I have enough money to try again if I fail the first time.

Timeframe = I think it will take me 40 hours to prepare for and pass the driving test. If I spend two hours a week then I'll spend 20 weeks or five months learning to drive.

Sun Tzu said: *A general is the leader of men; their fate is in his hands. In the best interest of the whole army, the general*

must be as objective as possible when dealing with a single soldier.

The aim of management should be to help people do a better job.

- It's management's task to remove the obstacles that prevent people from doing their jobs correctly.
- Only management is in a position to do something about the vast majority of errors.
- It is management's job to work continually on the system (for example work design, incoming work, improvement of tools, supervision, training and retraining). There is no stopping point in the process of quality management.

Think wisely, plan accordingly, and lead yourself into victory on every front.

III. Attack by Stratagem

Sun Tzu said: *In the art of war, it is better to capture the enemy whole and intact; if you destroy it then you have won but lost the prize. The General who has mastered the art of war will destroy as little as possible in order to win, keeping as many things of value intact as possible.*

Tim as Scrum Master wants to encourage his team to work faster and do better, so he setup competition for the best member of the team. By doing this he has encouraged the behavior of the superstar developer, which actually causes problems in a Scrum team. When competition begins in a team it moves them away from the concept of working collaboratively and instead pits one member against the other.

By doing this, Tim has destroyed the good feeling and collaborative energy that was there. Tim has replaced it with a poisonous competitive environment, which didn't help the team perform optimally.

Instead, Tim should look to find ways to encourage team work and collaboration. Team bonding meals and drink will help make the team stronger.

Buying donuts for the team to celebrate a good sprint is a simple yet effective way of encouraging team work and saying thank you.

Sun Tzu said: *Do not consider yourself a great general of* *high excellence if you have to fight in order to conquer. You are elite if you win instead by breaking the enemy's spirit and resistance without laying down a single fighting blow. The ideal is to prevent the enemy from executing its plan. Second best is to stop enemy forces from being deployed. Only if this fails must you engage the enemy on the battlefield. The worst policy is to lay siege to enemy city walls. Laying siege to the enemy's city walls will be a costly exercise that will take many months and will consume much of your resources.*

Getting the backlog written and the software developed can be done in many ways.

Being confrontational and pushy should be a last resort when striving to achieve a desired result. It is better to look at ways to create a truly collaborative environment where the product owner comes to stand up and feels ready to add his or her input. Testers are asking questions to the product owner or BA in a way that is trying to find the best solution.

Think about exploring options for building the product backlog.

Scope does not creep – Understanding grows.

It's much more important to think as a team and that is why it is key that all people in the standup are facing the scrum board. This is a way to ensure that all people are on the same side and the battlefield is the scrum board.

Sun Tzu said: *A general who is not able to control his emotions will be easily angered into launching an attack, the result of which is that 30 percent of his men will be killed and the city will remain untaken.*

When developing the software we should always look to think objectively rather than through the colorful lens of your emotions.

When the product owner wants to add something to the backlog then they need to be shown that something else must be dropped out to accommodate it. It should not be an emotional activity, but one of logic where we have a fixed capacity and different product backlogs must shuffle in and out.

Developer and tester should complement each other when working on building the software rather than it being a battle of passing over something that was half written.

A healthy environment should be created to facilitate and encourage a good working arrangement. Simply sitting together can aid in making this happen.

Sun Tzu said: *A skilled general will render the enemy's troops inert without any fighting, take their cities without laying siege to them, and plan for and conduct a victorious, short campaign.*

Before trying to put a new agile strategy to the team, you should ask the team. Getting the buy in from the team and the product owner is key to getting new initiative started.

It also makes sense to talk to other people in the organization to get a feel for how they have dealt with a similar problem or challenge.

Think about the best route to take and run a retrospective to decide where the best starting place is.

Sun Tzu said: *A general who can win without losing a single man and thus keep his forces intact is of elite standard. He has mastered the method of engaging the enemy with the use of strategy.*

When one is looking to adopt agile in a new environment, one should try to ensure that it is done at a pace that keeps everyone in the team onboard. A skilled scrum master will be able to moderate the pace, so that the team can move at a speed that they are able to make change, but not too quickly. What you want to so is implement Agile and not Fragile. You should think about bringing the team up to speed at a pace that covers the Tuckerman's stages of group development.

- Forming
- Storming
- Norming
- Performing

Forming is the stage where the team meets and learns about the opportunities and challenges, and then agrees on goals and begins to tackle the tasks. Team members are characterized by being positive and polite. Roles and responsibilities aren't clear and as scrum master you should help them get to know each other.

Storming people are beginning to push against the boundaries that were established in the forming stage. Many teams will fail at this stage if they are not helped to evolve. There will be conflict with people working styles and they will jockey for position in their roles. It is important that the scrum master takes time to help people get into the feeling of working as a collaborative team. Address issues when needed. Team members may have to be moved if they are disruptive.

Performing - the team can be considered to reach the performing stage when they are able to achieve their team goals without friction. The structure that has been set up then supports them in their goals. As a scrum master you can really focus on making the team even better.

Adjourning is the stage where the team is disbanded as the project has come to an end or there is restructuring happening. Before a team gets here it is good to see if a new set of teams can be built from the Adjourning team e.g. 4 scrum members may split out to create 4 new teams with the knowledge spread across a wide area of the organization.

Sun Tzu said: *In war one should consider one's numerical position. If one has 10 times as many resources as the enemy then he can surround him. If five times as many resources he can fight him, but if one has only twice as many resources then he should divide his resources into two parts.*

Available resources often dictate which actions can be taken. When thinking about how may stories your team can complete you should consider limiting the work in progress. The best way to do this is to visualize the work that the team is doing. Build a Kanban/scrum board for your team so that everyone can see what work is in progress.

By visualizing the work in progress you will be able to see the steps the team has to follow to get work done. Visually tracking your work on the board will create the wonderful benefits of transparency, focus and collaboration.

By visualizing your work it will help you to see where the resources are best placed. You might see that a developer is stuck on a user story and needs help - you can then ask him to do some pair programming to move things along faster.

By setting WIP limits you are increasing flow and when you are not setting WIP limits you are decreasing flow.

WIP limits can prevent the penalties of wasted time, effort and resources.

Sun Tzu said: *If one's forces are equally matched then he can engage the enemy. However if he has fewer forces he should avoid his enemy. If he is much smaller then he should retreat from him.*

Depending on the size of your resources and the task at hand, you have three choices:

1) Attack
2) Avoid and Hide
3) Retreat

If you have enough resources then you should be able to comfortable deliver the items in the backlog, which included Must have, Should have and Could have.

If you have fewer resources then you might have to de-scope items in the Could have.

If you have much smaller resources then you should focus you efforts on the Must have.

It is also important to think about what you are trying to achieve overall with your delivery and if you are really squeezed then you should do a story mapping exercise with the product backlog to see what really matters.

Sun Tzu said: *Despite occasional exceptions to the rule, a smaller force will very likely lose to a larger force.*

If you team is too small for the work that has been arranged in the backlog then you will need to increase the number of people, otherwise the delivery will be in danger. Agile can help to build a better product and improve productivity, but you have to have a balance with what can be done and what is impossible.

The other actions that might be tried are ways to see efficiencies in the team by pair programming, limiting work in progress and automation.

Sun Tzu said: *A country that has a strong general will be safe from his enemy but a country that has a weak general will be open to attack.*

Your success in the physical world is a manifestation of your inner world (i.e., your thoughts and beliefs). To become successful you must learn to control your thoughts and beliefs for they create your reality.

This is why it is critical to have a good Scrum Master in the team, which can not only facilitate discussion but can also protect the team and drive home the delivery. Getting your team to visualize that success is a useful exercise which will help them move towards their goal.

A team that is protected and well-motivated by good leadership will flourish and outperform. A team that is unprotected and under pressure will be demotivated and will fail to deliver what was needed. It is the job of Scrum Master to create an environment that maximized the motivation of the team.

Be like the strong general and act in ways that you know will lead to success, not stress.

Sun Tzu said: *A poor general can bring misfortune upon his army in three ways:*

(1) A General who commands his army to retreat or advance,

when they are not able to do so. This is called handicapping the army.

(2) When a General commands his army like his ruler governs his kingdom, when ignorant of their condition and circumstances. This causes agitation in the soldiers' minds.

(3) Commanding his officers without thinking of their situation and with ignorance of military principle. This will then shake the self-confidence of the soldiers.

Don't ask yourself or those around you to do the impossible.

Don't try to use one solution to fit all situations.

Don't repeat the same action regardless of the situation.

Don't ask your team to program more quickly if they are blocked or are impeded.

Don't expect people to pick up Agile without some training and coaching from an Agile Coach/Scrum

Master. Get the training you need before you apply Agile in order to ensure your success.

Try to ensure that the team work with the product owner or business analysis to understand what is being asked for.

Ask the tester to work with the business analysis to build and analyse test cases.

Sun Tzu said: *When the army is restless and lacking in unity they will be easily influenced and led astray by others. When there is a lack of unity then anarchy has a chance to seed itself and grow, thus destroying any chances of victory.*

Teamwork is a vital ingredient for success in any project or task. This is true not only in software development but in most aspects of life.

Look to create a win-win situation in which all participants benefit.

Win-win situations increase your success potential because of the positive network of opportunities they create. Those who have worked with you in any capacity and found you to be dependable and professional are much more likely to refer you for opportunities that arise in the future, some of which you otherwise may not have known existed.

When the product owner, business analyst, developer and tester are working as a single unit by collaborating, then the success level is high.

It is important to clear the path by having retrospective and standup - so members of the team do not diverge too far away.

We should always look to have frequent meetings to show and demo the software and encourage regular conversation. Too many contracts and documents build a wall and create opportunities of misunderstanding and ill feelings.

Sun Tzu said: *There are five essentials for victory:*

(1) Knowing when to fight and when not to fight.

(2) Knowing how to manage superior and inferior forces and resources.

(3) Knowing how to instill strength and honor in all of your forces.

(4) Planning and preparation, and then waiting to take on the enemy when he least expects it.

(5) Acquiring enough resources and firepower for the job but also being clear about your objective.

Anyone can be successful if they follow each of these steps:

(1) Know when to take action and when to stop and change course.

(2) Know how to apply the resources you have against the situation at hand.

(3) Know how to work well with other people. Learn to be a people person.

(4) Keep learning and adding to your skill set and apply those skills in surprising ways.

(5) Gather your resources; acquire a broad range of skills so that your team is highly cross-functional.

Sun Tzu said: *If you know yourself and know your enemy then you need not fear the result of one hundred battles. If you know yourself but not the enemy then you may suffer a defeat for every victory you win. If you know neither your enemy nor yourself then you will succumb in every battle.*

Know your team strengths and also their weaknesses, then play to their strengths and reduce the negative impact of their weakness. If they can master and work well with these two aspects then they will be much more successful in all they do.

If your team don't know the area they are going into, then they will suffer from set-backs and defeat. When this happens use each defeat to learn what will make them wiser and stronger as they gather their forces to try a new tactic.

The more you know about the terrain and the stronger your capabilities, the better your project delivery will be. Running workshops and retrospective will help discover things about your team that you can look to improve on.

Focus on what is going well, what is not going well and what you should keep doing.

IV. Tactical Dispositions

Sun Tzu said: *A skilled soldier puts himself beyond the possibility of defeat and then patiently waits for the right moment to strike and defeat the enemy.*

Before you engage in any project, or task assess the associated risks and how to minimize them. By putting yourself beyond defeat and waiting for the chance to defeat the enemy you set yourself up for the best vantage point from which to engage. When you estimate stories and place a size on them you are squeezing out the risk by helping the team understand what the story is about. You should look to include development, testing and business in these discussion rather than just taking an estimate from the developers.

Sun Tzu said: *Secure yourself against defeat by your own hands, but wait for the enemy to provide the opportunity for his own defeat.*

Train your team and be prepared to take action when the ideal opportunity arises. When opportunity meets preparedness, good things happen. People often call that being lucky.

Be the change you want to see. If you want to be a manager, behave like a manager. If you want your team to be more Agile then you need to create more agility by being a role model for agile values.

Read books written by other agile people, join agile forums and attend agile workshops and agile seminars that engage you and expand your knowledge and put you in the ranks you want to join. Set up special TDD/BDD sessions for your team and see if they can attend after hour sessions.

If you team has the chance, get them to listen to motivational speakers and emulate the successful attributes they expound. A winning Agile team is part tech, part attitude and a lot of hard work and motivation.

Sun Tzu said: *A skilled soldier may be able to make his position unassailable but he cannot be certain of defeating his enemy.*

Your team can prepare to the best of their abilities when working on the user story and execute the story as it has been written down, but there will always be the chance that it was not implemented as expected. To avoid this the product owner needs to be involved in reviewing the work that was done for the user story.

To maximize the chances of success your team need to continue to practice their agility by engaging with the product owner on a regular basis and not just at the sprint demo.

Sun Tzu said: *A person may know how to conquer but without being able to do so when it comes to putting theory into practice.*

Even if you know an area well and can execute your plan flawlessly, the environment in which you operate may not be conducive to your success. A team can be hampered when they are put into a non-agile environment. If the team is far away from the scrum board or the product owner has no time to meet on a regular basis then no matter how good the team is it will suffer.

Good Agile is about the team and environment – to adopt Agile you should always clear the way so that the team can be as effective as possible.

Sun Tzu said: *To prevent the enemy from defeating you, use defensive tactics; to beat the enemy go on the offensive.*

Both defensive and offensive approaches are important and one should work to master both. In order to win, however, you have to spend at least some time playing offense. Pursuing defensive tactics eventually only drains your energy and resources while it gets you nowhere. Being on the offensive, however, furthers your progress in reaching your goals, giving you the increased energy and motivation you need to continue to press on towards victory.

Richard was a scrum master for team Zebra and he always played defensive. He let things happen to him and his team rather than being proactive about changing the environment to be what he needed for his agile team. Richard let the team environment shape his team performance.

Samantha is a great scrum master because she looked to play offensive. She is proactive about getting the team into new Agile practices as soon as her boss mentions them.

She even takes the initiative to suggest new practices to her boss – getting the support needed for the Agile team. She encourages the Agile team to take their retrospective actions and track them on a Kanban board for the next sprint. She engages the Agile team and asks them, which of the retrospective action do the team really want to drive forward for the next sprint?

Samantha also encourages Agile learning practices by creating an Agile community of practice where like-minded people can share ideas across scrum teams. Different teams can share practices horizontally.

Sun Tzu said: *When you are of insufficient strength you may need to be on standby; but once you have an abundance of resources you can attack.*

When people play on the defensive, they normally lack something. Ask yourself and the Agile team if they lack any of the following:

- Self-belief or self-confidence
- Passion
- Energy

A shortage of any of these can impact the team's willingness or ability to go on the offensive and be more proactive. Identify your team's weaknesses in these areas and focus on improving them so that your team can acquire the confidence they need to effect positive change. High performing Agile teams have a high level of self belief, passion and energy.

Jason is a new junior developer lacking in self-esteem

and is very defensive about everything. He is socially withdrawn and very anxious around people. He lacks social skills and likes to keep to himself. He also expects little out of life. He is not very confident with his ideas and actions and tends to not follow through with anything. He lets things happen to him, and is miserable.

Rachel is a confident scrum master and has high self-esteem. She is talkative and loves to chat and socialize all the time. She is also a great listener and when she has an idea she follows through with it as efficiently as she can. She tends to make things happen and is always getting invited to do new things.

Rachel recognizes Jason's low self-esteem and tells him about classes on how to build self-confidence and encourages him to take them. She even helps him sign up for his first class and introduces him to a friend of hers who will also attend. Jason is surprised to learn at his first class that there are measured steps he can take to improve his ability to better handle social situations. Over the course of many months of classes he gains the skills to build his confidence level and finds he enjoys not only attending the classes but going out with new friends afterward.

Building an Agile team is not just about technical skills. It is about developing the team to be confident enough to ask the product owner questions. When teams make an assumption about a particular user story that is when we don't get the confirmation and fall back into a waterfall styled approach to software development. Team should also work on good old team build exercises.

Sun Tzu said: *The general who is a master of defensive strategies will hide himself and his forces, but a general who is a master of offensive strategies will launch an attack from sea, land, or from the heavens with lighting speed and precision. A master of defensive skills will be protective and a master of offensive skills will attack. He who knows both will have ultimate victory.*

In the Chinese philosophy of Taoism the yin-yang symbol represents shadow and light. This symbol shows how polar opposites are connected. One cannot be without the other. There is day and night, hot and cold, male and female.

Yin and yang are not opposing forces, but are complementary in nature.

Defensive and offensive skills represent complementary disciplines. When your team uses both well, a synergetic force is created which makes your team extremely powerful.

The yin-yang symbol is also symmetrical, which reflects the need for balance when using these disciplines. Too much defensive and too little offensive, or vice versa, will result in an unbalanced set of results.

Manuel, a new developer, works every waking moment on his current project at his new job. His boss loves him and his team admires him. It looks like Manuel is off to a great start to his career.

But Manuel has neglected to balance things, so his defensive side is weak. He hasn't eaten properly in weeks; he hasn't spoken to or seen his girlfriend in weeks, apart from the briefest of phone calls and a few texts. He also hasn't been sleeping much and is drinking tons of coffee.

Manuel gets a big pay rise and promotion from his boss, but the next day he doesn't show up at the office. His boss calls his cell and finds out Manuel is in hospital, recovering from exhaustion.

Remember an army marches on its stomach. Taking care of yourself is a form of defense that must be practiced on a regular basis.

Sun Tzu said: *A general who is able to win a battle when he has numerical superiority cannot consider himself elite.*

A leader's victories carry no accolades for wisdom or courage when the bar is set too low.

When your Agile team is comfortable in life they are probably not growing because they are not challenging themselves. Your team can only be as successful as their current levels of knowledge and skill will allow.

Look beyond your team's comfort level and strive for more. Take chances; set your team goals that challenge them. When your team reaches one target, focus on the next level and work towards that new goal.

Ken is a great database developer but has poor UX skills, which is holding the team back because they have to wait until Phil who has the key UX skill is back from his summer holidays. Ken should be encouraged to extend himself so that he can also work with the UX developer so that he can broaden his skill base to include some UX experience.

Jessie is a great tester but she uses the manual route for testing, she should spend time working on her automation skills and look into using an automated script tool such as selenium or QTP. Jessie could get involved in BDD and Gherkin to help the team move toward better testing practices. Jessie would benefit if she joined a community of practice for automation testing in the organization.

Big things are the result of a lot of small steps which can

only happen by taking time to make the first step.

Agile is a journey of learning and applying what works and letting go of what doesn't. It is an empirical process which the team must move through with the help of the scrum master and Agile Coach.

Sun Tzu said: *A general who wins his battles and is pronounced a genius is not one just because his nation calls him one. A general should be considered a genius or elite only when his actions have shown his worth.*

To pick up an autumn leaf is not a sign of great strength. To see the moon on a winter's night is not a sign of good sight. To hear the coming of a storm from the rage of thunder is not a sign of a keen ear.

Don't sell your team short. They are capable of doing great things, things that they have never believed were possible. Look at each day and recreate it anew. Do not strive for ordinary or second best, but strive for the best within yourself.

At the same time, be realistic about their resources and abilities, their strengths and weaknesses, the areas in which they need to improve in order to succeed as well as the areas in which they naturally excel.

Richard is a new BA on the team and wants to try a new way of doing things with the other scrum team members. Richard is keen to use story mapping for helping to engage the business and the rest of the scrum team. Without the help and encouragement of the other people in the team, he won't be able to succeed. Tom the scrum master should champion these Agile gems and facilitate and encourage the exploration of story mapping within the team and the wider audience.

Team Ruby does not have a full time scrum master. Instead they have a technical lead called Paul who is filling in for the scrum master role. Paul doesn't feel he has the authority to call on the BA team to look into story mapping and he is not able to engage business either. They do scrum but it feels very much a one way process and very internal to themselves.

To be a great team they should have a great scrum master who can build bridges with all the major players in the project.

Sun Tzu said: *To be called the title of elite one should not only have victory but should gain it with ease.*

When a great general wins his battles due to making no mistakes then his certainty of victory is sure to follow from that. The enemy's defeat was laid as soon as the general made his position unassailable.

A skillful general makes sure he positions himself so that defeat is impossible and then looks for the first moment in which he can defeat his enemy.

You can't anticipate and compensate for every possible mistake you may make or each surprise obstacle that may appear in your way, but you can focus on taking one step at a time toward your ultimate goal.

And that requires planning. It is better to execute an average idea brilliantly than to execute a brilliant idea poorly. Be systematic and methodical in your approach at all levels. Agile is not about being random but looking to see what works and building on that and ensuring that the team have a systematic way of delivering great working software.

Agile success is often obtained when excessive preparation leads to easy execution. Wise preparation is critical to success. This does not mean we should do big up front design and documents, but it means we should have lots of conversations and workshops in order to create a well-stocked product backlog. Good preparation should be done per sprint basis so each sprint goes really well. This means you need to be constantly grooming the product backlog with the product owner or BA.

Tina is the BA for the project, but she does not spend much time grooming the product backlog once the stories are written. Tina considers them well written and thus good enough for the team. She feels that her work is complete and moves onto a new project. Team Nexus struggles to understand and implement the stories she has written and now Tina is not available during the sprint. Team Nexus cannot ask her questions as she is busy with another team. This is blocking the team from getting the sprint stories completed.

Compare this to Tom who is the BA for Team Hero. Tom spends at least a few hours a day working on several of the user stories in the product backlog which are going to appear in the next sprint. Tom gets involved with the developers and testers when he is grooming the user stories so that he feels that the they are good enough for the sprint. Richard, their Scrum master, asks Tom if they are sprint ready and Tom is keen to see what the developers and testers think. Richard calls in a User story workshop session so that they can estimate and grade the user stories.

Richard and Tom work through the user stories and put sizing on them by playing planning poker. They check with the team and grade the stories from 1 to 10.

1 - the stories need more work.

10 – the stories are ready to go.

To jazz things up, the team match the lemon picture to the stories that need more work and place them on the visual scrum board. The ones that are ready to go are marked with the strawberry picture, meaning sweet and juicy. It's a fun and visual way for the team to keep track of what stories need more work and which ones are ready to go.

Sun Tzu said: *A master strategist will only seek to engage in battle when victory has already been won first in the mind and he need only execute his plan. A general who is destined for defeat will fight first and analyze the situation later.*

An Agile team should put effort into preparation of the product backlog and their release planning session. Being Agile does not mean not having a plan or not making preparations because the best teams will be continuously working on their backlog grooming. Doing this will stack the odds in your favor. They should focus on squeezing risk out by tackling the difficult user stories early rather than the simple ones. What your team wants is a lot of strawberry stories and no lemon ones.

Tips on stacking the odds in your favor:

- Groom the backlog often – daily if possible

- Make sure all stories are estimated
- Include testers and developers when writing stories and estimating
- Visualize work in progress
- Use color and pictures to enhance your visual board
- Do pair programming and use pairing matrix
- Collaborate often - daily is best

Sun Tzu Said: *A supreme general who follows the moral law and strictly observes method and discipline will thus be gifted the power to control success.*

Work to align your team's inner and outer mission and apply a systematic methodical approach to joining the two. When you fuse your team's inner world with your team's outer world you are much more likely to achieve extraordinary success.

Inner world desire: Your team dream of becoming extremely Agile through following as many Agile practices as possible. They also look to use as many of the Agile tools to improve their performance.

Outer world reality: Your team are working in an

environment where management have not yet adopted Agile from the top downwards. They are still funded in a waterfall way and management are still looking to do big up front designs and requirements.

If your team are to truly succeed then they need to work on the inner world as well as get buy-ins from management.

Agile anti pattern, which are to be avoided:

- no funding for white boards
- no place to put the whiteboards
- stationary is restricted for post-it notes and marker pens.
- There are not enough meeting rooms
- There are no drop in meeting rooms
- There are no writeable walls in the building
- The team and product owner are not co-located
- no room in the office to allow for pair programming (poor desk space allocation/monitors)
- no code reviews
- no place to do a stand up around the white board

- stand up happens in the corridor with a small tiny whiteboard
- management do not want to waste time sprint planning
- sprint review are not done because business is too busy
- sprint review cant be done as there is no projector/Monitor/laptop in meeting room
- no retrospective is done as there is no support from management for the time they take.
- management interrupting the scrum team during the sprint to ask them to do some other important work / context switching with new important stories being added in mid sprint
- Team being self directed without guidance from management to set goals and provide Agile containers of sprint planning, stand up etc.
- no funding for decent laptops / pc's
- no funding for latest Agile software tools and licenses
- no funding for training for agile courses

Sun Tzu Said: *In method of warfare we first must consider the attribute called Measurement, then Estimation of quantity, then Calculations followed by Balancing of the chances and, finally, Victory.*

To be successful in your Agile adoption you need to measure your agility. Agile is an empirical process of setting small experiments, taking a measurement and then calculating if this has had the desired effect and adapting the process so that the team can pivot to victory.

Some form of measurement is needed in order to assess success. In Agile you have to be careful of what you want to measure.

Take, for example, an IT help desk which is setup to support a business. They measure how many tickets they have closed every week. What this leads to is help desk staff closing tickets quickly by providing the minimum amount of help which creates the behavior of closing the ticket even if the issues have not been properly resolved.

Example:

Adam is a helpdesk guy who has someone call him about Outlook not working properly. Adam tells the user to reboot the machine and then closes the call down. With the helpdesk ticket having the description filled in with the text - the machine required a reboot. They may not have properly fixed the problem but the pressure is for Adam to close his ticket by his 2 hr SLA rather than the old 3 day SLA.

He is happy for the customer to call again and ask them to open a new ticket for the issue that the person is facing.

The system behavior changes because Adam had to respond to a 2 hour SLA rather than a 3 day SLA. He needs to act as quickly as possible, which might not have been the best action for the person involved. The help desk seems to be more efficient but it not really meeting it purpose of helping people. A better measure would have been to take a follow up call to the person and ask if they are happy with the service and keep the SLA to a workable timeframe.

The helpdesk manager focused solely on a measure that didn't relate directly to the whole customer service experience. In the end the helpdesk met their goal and possibly made customer service worse.

Agile Dashboard:

- Completed / Committed Stories. % Ratio

Below 75% or above 125% would be flagged as poorly planned.

So during the past 4 sprints:

0 poorly planned sprints = Excellent

1 = Good

2 = Average

3 = Watch

4 = Bad

This will allow us to track planning health.

- Sprint Velocity - We track the last 4 sprint velocities and show the %Change
- Niko-niko Calendar - This is a daily calendar which tracks the mood of each team member over each day of the sprint. Ratio of happy to sad faces should be greater than 50%. We want the team to be more happy than sad over the sprint.

Individual and group behaviors will evolve to meet your measures – not necessarily your goals. The key is to ensure that the measures you use promote the behaviors you desire.

Another area to consider for measurement is waste - the opposite of productivity.

Waste #1 – partially done work

This could be work that cannot be demonstrated to

customers or cannot be released.

Reasons:

- Removing a story that is in progress in the current sprint and replacing it with a different story. *(Track No. of stories replaced in sprint)*

- Prioritizing a story into the current sprint without understanding the story completely from the product owner. *(Track stories dropped due to going into sprint before they were sprint ready)*

- Story was not properly analyzed in the sprint planning and possibly not really estimated in a collaborative way i.e. one of these people were missing in the session (dev, tester, ba) or dev only estimates. Scrum master only estimates. *(Track No. stories analyzed by full team)*

- Wait time in between task due to team needing to go back to a busy product owner. *(Track No. of days waiting for reply to question from PO – you can draw banana icons next to the user story on the scrum board. 1 banana for 1 day worth of waste due to waiting for a reply from the product owner)*

- Dependencies in the story to another story in the backlog. *(Track No of stories drop or stopped due to being dependent on other user story sitting in product backlog)*

Waste #2 – Extra Features

Gold-plating the solution is something that is going to create waste. What you want is to implement the minimum viable set of features which produces the outcome or goals that are desired. More features does not mean better product or better selling product. It just means a product that is bloated. What customers really want are products that meet their needs.

Reason:

- Product Owner not creating a clear vision document and not doing customer focused workshops to validate the vision document. Don't build what you think they want - build what they really want! Good Agile is all about getting early feedback on the product - it is not about throughput. It is not about the go faster stripe, it is about doing less work and getting more of what the customer wants. (*Track understanding by building story maps*)

- Not creating personas and thinking about the customer bases. The team should work with the product owner and build a set of personas that represent the market audience. (*Track personas created for the product and who works on it*)

- Gold plating the architecture by over engineering the code to account for scenarios that may never happen. (*Track design evolution so that it starts out as simple as it needs to be to support the product backlog stories.*)

Waste #3 Relearning

This is when we are not using the knowledge that we have gained from a previous session and the effect of this is re-inventing the wheel.

Reason:

- A Successful Agile team is disbanded once the project is over rather than keeping them for the next project. (*Keep good Agile team going and if you need to break them, split them to seed new teams. Only disband a non performing agile team*)
- Too busy delivering software and not running retrospective and doing retro actions. (*Time should be set aside for retrospectives and their actions*)
- Not leveraging and learning from other scrum teams. (*Set up communities of practices to ensure an agile eco system is being built, which will leverage that knowledge*)

Waste #4 Hand off

This is when one person finishes his task and then passes on the story to another person.

Reason:

- Team members working in different time zones (*If possible collocate teams or use WebEx Calls*)

- Team members working in different locations (*If possible collocate teams or use WebEx Calls*)

- Team members having different skill sets i.e. a not so cross functional team. (*You should look to encourage the team to be cross functional by doing more pairing of team members*)

Waste #5 Delays

Delays happen when more time is added to the value add activities or there is a greater lead time before the value add activity can begin

Reason:

- Unwanted Processes (*Agile is about being empirical which means we learn from the evidence. We should only have enough processes to meet the need and only add more when we find that evidence shows that we need to add to the process to make it better*)

- Too many things in progress (*Agile Team should look to limit the work in progress in their sprints so that we can finish what we have started. It is better to have 3 finished stories that 13 unfinished ones.*)

- Lack of required team members (*When we have an*

Agile team that does not have required team members then waste occurs as we have to find the right people to help or spend a long time trying to gain the required skills)

Waste #6 Task Switching

- Interruption due an ongoing tasks. (The *Scrum master should protect the team from getting interrupted*)
- A team which is working on more than one project at one time. (*Programme manager should look to align one team to one work stream*)
- Late analysis of the task for the required story *(Business Analyst/Designer should be involved in creating enough support knowledge for the user story*)
- Poor co-ordination between product owner and development team. (*Scrum Master should make sure that there is effect collaboration between product owner and development team*)

Waste #7 Defects

This is an erroneous functionality that produces the wrong output

- The story does not satisfy the INVEST Principle

(The team should look to get the story aligned to the INVEST principle as much as possible. If the story was not estimated and put into the sprint then chances are that there was not enough understanding around the story. If the story was not small enough then the team didn't break it down and there was not enough understanding around the story. If acceptance criteria was not thought about properly then the story was not well understood.)

- Lack of understanding of the story *(This is the symptom of not enough grooming. The team should look to groom the story and make sure that it has been estimated and meets a sprint-ready criteria)*

- Lacking Engineering Practices (*If the team has not used rigorous engineering then defect can creep in. Your team should look to do code review, pair programming, refactor often and use TDD*)

- Missing Acceptance Criteria (*If the team has not been able to talk to the product owner about how the story will be tested and qualified as done then issues will occur. The team should not take on a story until the end state has been understood.*)

- Lack of involvement from the testers (*The Scrum master should look to involve the testers from the beginning of the project and at all points in delivery rather than just at the end of the sprint.*)

- Not enough automation (*As the team mature in*

their Agile practice they should look to see if they can bring more and more automation onto the scene.)

- Missing technical skills from the team (*The Scrum Master should look to ensure that the team grow in a cross functional way through pair programming and collaboration exercises.*)

Sun Tzu Said: *Measurement owes its existence to Earth, Estimation of quantity to Measurement, Calculation to Estimation of quantity, Balances of chances to Calculation, and Victory to Probabilities.*

Note the dependant nature of victory. Victory must be defined. Without such a definition, how does one know if he's succeeded or not?

When you define victory you bring yourself closer to it because you can make an informed judgement as to what you need to do in order to achieve it. If you just take action without understanding what victory requires, then you could be using your resources in places in which it is not helping you to be successful.

The Agile Coach should help the business work:

What does success look like? What does a great Agile Team look like? What does a great Agile Space look like?

What does an Agile organization look like?

- Do the team members collaborate often or do they work in silos?
- Do the team members ask critical questions to the product owner or do they have a one way relationship with the product owner?
- Does the Agile team have regular stand up meetings and a big visible information radiator?
- Does the team feel free to experiment with new ideas such as TDD/BDD or do they have constant pressure to deliver software?
- Does the team have a team space where they can work through ideas and really own that space?
- Does the product owner look at the scrum board with the team and consider what can be done better rather than talking to the team?
- Does the organization look to build great software or record a lot of team metrics?
- What are the key metrics that really matter for the definition of success? Velocity? Fun? Defects? Explore the factors that matter for the business and the Agile team.

Choose a measure, choose the quantity for that measure, determine what calculations produce that quantity and what chances work with your calculations, and finally understand that those outcomes reveal if victory is yours or not.

As an Agile Coach, work with teams and organizations to find out what measures are to be captured and why they matter. The Agile Coach should also help to see how these measures aid the improvement of Agile delivery.

Sun Tzu Said: *A winning army compared to a failed one is like a lead weight place in the balancing scales against a single grain.*

Defeat is demoralizing and weighs upon the soul, while victory uplifts the victor and energizes him to further successes. Choose your measure of success wisely because if it truly tests you it will take much effort to achieve. When you do achieve it, however, enjoy the spoils.

Team Zebra have been working hard to increase their velocity form the last sprint which was only 15 points. Their Agile Coach Paul had asked them to think of a number of things which they could do to make the team perform more efficiently. The team have come up with 3 things that they like to do to lift their efficiency.

- Raise their team morale by having mid sprint – team lunches.

- Pair up when a team member gets blocked and stuck on a User Story.
- Limit their work in progress to no more than 3 user stories.

In the Second Sprint, Team Zebra were able to deliver 26 points because they limited themselves to taking on no more than 3 stories and pairing up to break the back of one of the difficult ones. Their team morale was much higher and their stress levels were lower after having a team lunch to discuss all the difficulties they had encountered in week 1 of the sprint and what they might do to get all the stories completed in week 2.

Team Hydra wanted to impress those around them and decided to commit to 6 user stories ,which were all sized at 8,8,13,13,20,20 point stories for a total of 82 points. They were only able to complete 2 of the 6 because they had taken on too many large stories – two size 8 were completed for a total velocity of 16 - the rest of the stories were work in progress. Team Hydra would have been better off focusing on limiting the work in progress and trying to get more stories completed, than looking to just pick a lot of bigger sized stories. By purely focusing on story points they delivered less completed stories and left a lot of work in progress, which were the 2 x 13 and 2 x 20 stories.

Sun Tzu Said: *The rush of conquering forces should be*

likened to the bursting of water from a dam cascading down a chasm a thousand feet deep.

When your Agile team succeeds in an area on which they have set their ambitions, they should feel the rush and exhilaration of being alive. A team's velocity should not be the only driving force for victory—passion should be that force. Velocity should simply provide a way to keep score of how well your Agile team is doing.

V. Energy

Sun Tzu said: *The control of a large resource requires the same principles as the control of a smaller resource; it is merely a question of dividing up their numbers.*

Success often requires that you first learn to manage a project on a small scale and then exponentially increase your efforts to build the size of that project while also increasing your skills and ability to manage things well.

When looking to make changes in the Agile team these can be done without pomp and ceremony because a team needs to explore different ways to increase their agility. If an Agile change is rolled out to 50 teams in one go, it will be difficult to manage that change until it has been proven on a smaller scale. Let one team try out a new idea and then propagate that to another team through the community of practice or show casing. It is important that the Agile team feels that they can experiment and explore, rather than being given hard and fast changes that have to be implemented. There should be a framework because Scrum has always been about getting the team to fill in the details to some extent, rather than it being a recipe book of instructions to follow.

Sun Tzu Said: *To employ a large army is no different from using a regiment; it is a matter of instituting signals and signs.*

Establish a system through which you issue orders and those under you follow them. A staff training manual should be equally useful whether you have one staff member or 100 staff members. It is important that each member of the team and any person who is working on an Agile project should receive agile training. It is very easy for one person who is not working in an agile way to disrupt the delivery of a critical project. For example, a BA who is used to working in a waterfall way could cause bottlenecks and blockage in the delivery. The BA may be writing user stories and even using the BDD syntax for his stories, but if he is not collaborating with the team and only work with the product owner then he is really not helping the project that much. The team will just receive a bunch of user stories which are less useful than a full BRD because the BA does not have the time to sit with the team to bring the user stories alive and for the team to ask questions.

An organization can raise their Agility by ensuring that all members of the team have Agile training so that they can become more collaborative. When the product owner or BA does not go to the stand up, this also weakens the agility of the team. Likewise, when a single member starts to miss the standup then it also weakens the team.

All team members should attend and contribute to the retrospective so that the team can ensure that they are continuously improving. When someone in the team does not want to attend the retrospective then it weakens the retrospective and makes it less valuable. When team members do not follow through with their retrospective actions during the next sprint, it will also weaken the team's ability to continuously improve.

These rituals are there to build strength in the team in the same way that regular exercise builds strong muscles in the body.

The team and product owner should attend the review to ensure that everyone knows what was done in the sprint that has just finished. When someone does not attend it - it sends out the message that people don't care about the product that they are creating. This should not happen and it is important that people attend these meetings to keep the passion alive for the product. Simple things make these meetings go well, such as drinks and snacks, and also keeping the meeting short and to the point.

The visual board is the key to the heart of an Agile team and should be decorated with all the team efforts. They should see where team members are – using avatars is a great way of achieving this. Using other signs, such as stop signs for blockages and traffic lights for RAG reporting, is also great for helping people see what is happening on the board. Using color to help coordinate the team is also extremely useful. Different color post-it notes can be used to categorize different actions or dependencies.

- Pink Post-It notes could be used for interruptions
- Orange Post-It notes could be used for bugs
- Yellow Post-It notes could be used for team tasks
- Blue Post-It notes could be used for external tasks.

The Scrum Master and team should spend time optimizing their board, as this will be a major key asset in helping the Agile team succeed.

Sun Tzu Said: *Use maneuvers that are direct and indirect to ensure you can withstand the brunt of an enemy's attack.*

For an Agile Team to get software delivered they need to look at tackling the product backlog directly and being honest and transparent about what will work and what will not work. But like all great Agile teams, if they need to ask permission to do every little thing then the ability to be 'Kaizen' is diminished. The team cannot explore and look for continuous improvement if they are hamstrung with all decisions. Therefore the best way to approach Agile transformation is to provide a framework with boundaries for the team to work in but still remain flexible by offering the opportunity to discover better ways of being Agile through retrospective actions and coaching. For example, the daily stand up must happen every day and at a fixed time and duration, but the team has the option to experiment with different times to ensure that they are operating optimally. This does not mean the daily stand up keeps changing times every day, but it means the team should be able to decide that 9.15am doesn't work for them and they prefer 9.30am going forward.

Sun Tzu said: *The bearing of your army may be likened to that of dashing an egg against the grind stone – you must study the science of strong and weak points in all its forms.*

Try breaking an egg by squeezing it in the palm of your hand; it is extremely difficult to break one this way. However if you hit the egg on the side with the edge of a spoon then it will break quite easily.

To help teams become more Agile you should look to find engagement points where there is little resistance to change.

For example: Team Cobra had been using Agile for a few months now, but they found that their user stories had poor acceptance criteria, which caused them problems. Zach, their Scrum Master, introduced them to BDD (Behavioral driven development) and the Gherkin syntax. Zach was able to talk to the BAs and Tester about writing acceptance criteria and providing scenarios in this format.

Team Jade were having their daily stand up at 9.30am and this had been working very well for over a year, but one of the team members wanted to move it to 10.15am. The rest of the team did not want to move to the later date because it would mean that they started later on in the day. The team's resistance was high and it was better to keep to 9.30am as it was working better for most of the team.

Agile is about improvement by change rather than change without good reason for it.

Sun Tzu said: *A general can use a direct approach to enter into battle but if he wants to gain victory he must also know how to use an indirect approach.*

Forcing Agile practices onto teams is never as effective as getting the team to build Agility by letting them evolve what works well for them and letting the rest fall away.

This is much more true when you enter in the more advanced stages of an Agile team, but new incubator teams will need firm guidance.

Tom, the Scrum Master for Team Xendar, had to provide firm guidelines for his new team. They had only been assembled in the last week and they have not worked together in an Agile team before. Tom needs to set firm groundrules to ensure that the members participated in the daily standup, the sprint review and sprint retrospectives. As the team progresses, Tom lets the team experiment more with their processes, but for the first few months they need to build their confidence and processes with what was core.

Sun Tzu said: *Indirect tactics can be used in limitless ways. They are as numerous as the stars in the night sky and they are always renewing themselves like the change of the seasons.*

Ways to improve the Agility of the team are unending and ever-changing.

In the early 90s it was UP and DSDM, then followed by Scrum, Kanban and XP, which now leads us to DAD, SaFE and LeSS.

Teams should always look to find new and better ways to do Agile software development.

Sun Tzu said: *There are no more than five musical notes, yet the world is filled with more music than you can ever listen to in your lifetime.*

There are five Scrum values

- *Focus*
- *Courage*

- *Openness*
- *Commitment*
- *Respect*

If your Agile Teams are able to embrace each and every one of these scrum values then they would be able to deliver great, authentic software to the market. To get there, take care of not just the team but the participation of the whole organization.

Sandy, the Scrum Master of Team Reload, had spent many months working with the different parts of the organization to encourage openness, respect, commitment, courage and focus. She believes in the power of Agile being a mindset and not just a bunch of process improvement tips. Her mantra is 'be the change you want to see'. Agile for her is not just doing it but being it. Living Agile from day to day.

There are only five primary colors (red, blue, yellow, black, and white), but when combined they create an infinite number of colors, more than can ever been imagined.

There are not more than five basic tastes (salt, sweet, acrid, sour, and bitter) but when combined they create more flavors than a chef could ever dream of.

Simply collecting more and more IT skills will not make your team more successful due to the law of diminishing returns. How you use what you know is what really matters.

For example, Rik the Scrum Master for Team Quatron, encouraged the team to learn as many new IT Skills as possible. They learnt 3 new scripting libraries - Angular.JS, Backbone.JS, Ember.JS. In the next sprint they started to write code using all 3 libraries. Some team members use Anguar.JS, others used Backbone and Ember.JS.

This causes some problems with the team because not everyone was familiar with all 3 libraries and there was no consistent use of these JS Libraries.

The team would have been much better at discussing the project and what technology would be most useful in accomplishing their goal in that sprint. Had Rik helped them to do that then they could have come to a collaborative agreement to use Angular.JS instead of trying to use all 3 libraries.

The team would be better off focusing on gaining proficiency in one of these libraries for 6 months and then adding a new library if they really found that need to use it. That is the Agile way - inspect and adapt.

Agile teams should master a limited number of key skills and then apply them well. That is a key secret to a successful Agile team.

A computer has five basic instructions; to add, subtract, branch, store, and retrieve. Every amazing thing you see a computer do is built around those five basic instructions or skills.

An Agile team should master their basic key elements first before jumping to more advanced topics.

A lot of teams get caught up in wanting to acquire more skills or learn more things, hoping to uncover a secret Agile gold mine along the way. This is not necessarily a bad thing, but they should remember that the key is to learn to embrace the scrum core values.

Team members should look within themselves and remember that part of the key to their success lies within them. It is their self-belief that grants them victory. You cannot have success without doing something and applying yourself, and none of that is possible without self-belief.

Sun Tzu said: *There are only two styles of attack in battle, that is the indirect and the direct; when these two are arrangement they give rise to an unending series of maneuvers.*

The indirect and the direct follow each other in turn. It is like the turning of a wheel - It never comes to an end. Can anyone exhaust the possibilities of their combinations?

By applying all the different skills that your Agile team

have, they can produce an endless series of results. Look to your team's own inner well of strength and apply those skills when they are faced with each new challenging situation. As long as they have hope they will always have the chance for victory. The chance for victory is only lost when your team gives up hope.

Sun Tzu said: *When the army forces are released into battle it is likened to the torrent of water rushing down a mountain during a storm; even stone, mud, and wooden stumps are washed along its course.*

When your Agile team begins to adopt Agile there is always resistance, be it from themselves (an internal resistance) or from others (an external resistance). To be successful your Agile team must exert enough energy to break through such resistance. Once they have done that then the boulder that has been blocking their path begins to move slowly. To create a torrent of force your Agile team must keep that initial momentum moving by applying energy at a consistent level over a period of time.

It is better to apply a consistent small amount of energy over a long period of time than it is to apply a huge amount of energy over a short period of time.

Which person will move the boulder farthest? The person who exerts a consistent force over a larger period of time.

Look to make sure that your Agile transformation programme has enough time to work its magic. 6 months is not enough time to realize those gains, instead look to have a 3 year programme where you can drive change over multiple years rather than over a few months.

Sun Tzu said: *The quality of decision is like the well-timed swoop of an eagle which enables it to accurately strike and kill its victim.*

Focus your team's energies and make sure they are having the desired effect. Don't put out a lot of energy in an unfocused way. Conserve your team's energy and direct it in short but effective bursts.

There is not a linear relationship between the Agile team's effort used and the results produced. Doubling your team's effort doesn't always result in doubling your Agile team's success level.

A principle known as the Pareto principle, also known as the 80–20 rule, states that about 80 percent of effect comes from 20 percent of cause.

Successful Agile teams either consciously or subconsciously apply this principle though various aspects of their work. They maximize their efforts in the 20-percent area which then produces the 80-percent result they want. Successful Agile teams are not looking for perfection or 100-percent results. They are looking to maximize their results by expending the least amount of resources - limiting the work in progress or amount of work done - cutting out waste. That is not to say that they don't put effort into going that extra mile. Rather, it means the great Agile team focuses their efforts and by putting in that extra mile in the 20-percent area that will deliver the 80-percent result so that their chance of success is increased.

Sun Tzu said: *A good general will be slow at the beginning while circling his enemy, probing for weaknesses, but when striking he will be quick and accurate like the eagle.*

While assessing a situation, take your time to plot your best course, but once you've committed waste no time in taking action. Move swiftly and execute without second thoughts or hesitation. The Agile team should respond to change and be focused on targeting those user stories that really matter. An Agile BA can help in the matter by helping to focus the Agile team and product owner by using the story mapping technique to walkthrough what really matters.

Sun Tzu said: *Energy can be likened to the bending of a crossbow; decision, to the releasing of a trigger.*

Change is instant, like the releasing of a trigger.

The bending of a crossbow holds the energy required to move all obstacles out of the way so you are put in a position ready for change.

This energy is the mental preparation work or groundwork your Agile team needs to do that will put them in that state of readiness. The key, then, is to get your team in the correct mental state when it is time to release that energy and take action. A number of key Agile activities can be used to help create this mindset.

- Brown Bag Session (Lunch and learn)
- Retrospective Meetings
- Agile group training session and coaching sessions

To clear away any confusion or denial or any other distraction that can block your Agile team's chances for success, consider researching different types of psychotherapy than can help your Agile team understand and better control their mind-body connections.

Some people have found success with an approach known as neuro-linguistic programming (NLP), which can help one recognize what is blocking their efforts and get 'unstuck' so that they can instantly act and succeed. Replacing fear with images of a successful mentor in action can help you feel more confident, especially if you've spent a lot of time researching that person and his methods.

"The winners in life think constantly in terms of I can, I will, and I am. Losers, on the other hand, concentrate their waking thoughts on what they should have or would have done, or what they can't do." – Dennis Waitley

By focusing on the desired outcomes you can unlock the Key to creating high-performance and outstanding results in work and life.

Using NLP has been a tried and tested way of helping people achieve better results by getting them to focus on the outcomes.

- Visualize: what does a successful Agile transformation look like in your organization?
- Visualize: what does a successful Agile team look like in your department?
- Visualize: what does great business and technology collaboration look like in your organization?
- Visualize: what does a successful sprint review

look like in your software department?

The big break through in Agile goal setting:

When you want to go from A to B, it not just about doing A and then getting B. Your Agile team need to focus on B then they have to act as if they have B already.

If your Agile team want to be more collaborative then they need to act as if they are a highly collaborative team. Your Agile team needs to hold themselves to a higher standard. Don't send that email or defer that contact with the product owner - the Agile team should be comfortable with having interaction with the product owner - face to face.

That's why great Agile teams say that you have to **BE-DO-HAVE**, not HAVE-DO-BE.

The right Agile thought pattern is BE-DO-HAVE because then your Agile team's thoughts, feelings, and actions support your Agile team's end results.

Sun Tzu said: *In the heat of the battle there may seem to be disorder where there is in fact a plan. Among the chaos and confusion there is method to what appears to be madness.*

Sometimes your Agile team may feel many things are occurring at the same time and they are not making any progress. Especially in the early days of adopting Agile, such times can be trying for all involved. Your Agile team should keep in mind the big picture of their ultimate goal, even as they struggle to cope with a seemingly endless stream of small challenges.

Your Agile team need to keep the faith, the vision, and the big picture in mind, as they continue with determination to overcome the project obstacles and see the project through to its completion.

Sun Tzu said: *The clever fighter uses the power of combined energies and does not depend solely on the exceptional skills of any individual. He picks out the right people and teaches them to work together to create a greater effect.*

Being successful does not have to be an individual affair. You can achieve an even greater victory when you use the effort of many.

It is better to have a highly motivated cross functional team than a few lone hot shot programmers. When looking to have a great Agile team you should endeavor to create well rounded members in technical skills as well as their people skills.

A great collaborative Agile team is worth more than one great coder.

Gary is the Scrum Master for Team Yankee and he relied on one key software guy called Jason who carried all the weight. When Jason left for 3 weeks to get married, the team ground to a halt due to everyone depending on him. Jason was the single point of failure.

Sarah is the Scrum Master for Team Killer and she believes in getting everyone involved in driving the Agile project to success. Sarah encourages team work through active participation in all the key ceremonies.

Sun Tzu Said: *When a clever fighter uses the power of combined energy he can create a cohesive force that is like drops of rain falling on the leaves of a tree seemingly gentle and, when collected in force, able to smash trees and rocks. When it becomes a torrent, such a force can burst through a swollen river bank and destroy everything in its path.*

An Agile team must have a clearly stated goal or mission before it can unleash its full power to great effect.

Luke, the Scrum Master for team Jaxx, gets the team to visualize what a successful sprint looks like for the team. He also runs effective planning sessions, which help the team focus on what user stories add value and which one needs to be re-thought. Luke brings clarity by asking question to the product owner and team to ensure that everyone is in alignment with the sprint stories.

Helen is having difficulties as a Scrum Master, as she has

let the product owner Lucy do all the driving with the sprint backlog in the planning session. Lucy doesn't know what she wants and is unsure of what needs to happen to make the software do the wonderful thing she needs it to do. Lucy keeps chopping and changing her mind after the planning session was concluded and as a result the team has a lot of half finished work at the end of the sprint. Helen should have ensured that Lucy was clear on what is the sprint goal and how the chosen stories will enable that to happen. This is a conversation that Helen must have with the team to ensure everyone is on the same page.

Sun Tzu Said: *The energy developed by the cohesion of a united force can move trees and mountains. Such is the force of nature and unity.*

A set of skilled people working together to achieve a clear objective can do phenomenal things. Examples of this include the building of the pyramids, or NASA putting a man on the moon or a rover on Mars.

Getting your team to work together in a fully Agile way can reap wonders and might even put a man on the moon.

VI. Weak Points and Strong

Sun Tzu said: *When an army is first to the battlefield it will be fresh and ready for fighting. The army that comes second will rush to get into place and will be exhausted.*

Before your team takes on a new task or project, make sure you set them up to be successful at it. The Scrum master needs to provide the right kind of environment so that teams can become Agile.

As a Scrum Master you will need to keep the team fresh by helping to encourage an environment of learning and continuous improvement.

Watch for team burn out and ensure that they stay alert by making sure that they are running at a sustainable pace and are positively aligned about the tasks ahead.

Teams that do well exercise and eat well - so keep that in mind when getting the team to a high performance point.

Teams can strengthen their mind and spirit by reading motivational Agile books and cases studies of successful projects. Even listening to motivational speakers can provide a welcomed boost to the mind.

Planning the release well will prepare the team to take the delivery by the horn.

Scrum Master and Team should look to build a visual road map on the office wall so that they can see the progress and discuss it with key stakeholders.

Sun Tzu said: *A clever fighter will put his will onto his enemy but will not allow the enemy to do the same to him.*

It is not necessary as a Scrum Master to fight every battle that comes your way. Fight only the battles you can win on your terms.

Your Agile team should always be looking to choose favorable situations that allow them to grow their Agile foundation. Start with the small things when adopting Agile.

When getting stakeholders to the daily meeting you should look to invite those who are keen to collaborate, as they will become your advocates to the cause. They can help spread the good word to their colleagues.

When doing the planning session bring the product owner to the session and ask them to collaborate by reading out the user stories to the rest of the team and explaining what he or she wants. Give them some whiteboard and markers and then great things will happen. Product owners are naturally enthusiastic and want to tell everyone about what interests them rather than getting it to go the other way.

Product owners should also attend the review meeting and they can be strong advocates, so long as the meetings are short and to the point and provide them with touch points to tell the team about what was done well and other features that need more work.

Sun Tzu Said: *When marching through a territory that has no enemy the soldiers will be able to move great distances without any problems.*

As a Scrum master, keep an eye out for new and unexplored Agile opportunities and step in to fill a need the same way so many famous pioneers and innovators have done in the past. When building your visual Kanban board don't be boring and use the standard format - look to experiment with different ways of visualizing the work in progress. Using different magnetic symbols can be rewarding such as fruits - strawberry for tasks that are going well or the juicy user stories. Use banana magnets for user stories that are going to be tricky and the team needs to pay extra attention too.

Moving through uncharted territory requires immense self-belief because there are no sign posts and no one to follow. But the best opportunities can be found in such territory and its lack of limits, which allows much distance to be covered at a very fast pace. Sometimes you have to pioneer these Agile ideas in different environments, which some people may seem to find alien to begin with.

Sun Tzu said: *If you attack places that are undefended then you can be sure of victory and success. Likewise you would be wise to build your defenses so they are in an unassailable position.*

The world is always evolving and presenting new opportunities and frontiers. It is the ability to take on those undefined areas that provides us with a rich reward. It is important to run a number of retrospective to find out what aspect of Agile have been under developed.

Sun Tzu said: *The art of war requires knowledge of subtlety and secrecy; if you can master these skills then the enemy's fate is in your hands.*

When your Agile team first finds these new and unexplored places, your first instinct may be to rush off excited and tell everyone what you know about your new find. Keep your ideas under wraps until you have had a chance to experiment and gather data which can be used to strengthen your position in helping drive Agile adoption within the business. It takes time for Agile to flourish and a great idea can be killed off before it has had a chance to prove itself.

Sun Tzu: *If you target and strike at the enemy's weak points then you will be able to gain a great victory, and if you are swifter than him then you will always be out of harm's way.*

Sometimes the best way to get the most out of a new Agile idea is to move quickly with it. If you spot a gap in the organization, where you can, use and adopt it before others do in the market place.

The difference between moving quickly and moving slowly can be measured in the cost of millions of dollars of lost revenue or in ultimate victory.

Sun Tzu said: *If we are trying to avoid engaging in battle then we must look to put something unusual and peculiar in the enemy's way. This will make him stop and question the battlefield and this new variable.*

When looking to deliver great Agile software you should look to help the product owner see the wood through the trees. Help the product owner to visual the product backlog by mapping out the user story journey. By arranging stories in a story mapped way vs the product backlog list format, the product owner can see when a user stories position seems unusual or peculiar.

Sun Tzu said: *If we are able to create a cohesive force, while we cause the enemy to split up we will be able to conquer him.*

Divide and conquer. No matter how big or powerful a system is when divided it can be easily overcome. Consider a system's weakest link and attack it. Even a seemingly unbreakable force can be damaged via such a strategy. When looking to help an organization adopt Agile, there should be a large transformation program put in place which can work across the vertical with various CIOs and also horizontally in Community of Practices.

Look to have one Agile Coach pair with a CIO for the organization, such as a large financial institution.

Middle managers can help with building the community of practices.

Sun Tzu said: *We should keep the time and location of the engagement hidden from the enemy. This will mean the enemy will need to divide his force across several fronts. This will mean he is thinly spread across his borders.*

Before bringing Agile to the wider audience look to see a good level of Agile adoption at the ground across all

CIOs verticals.

Manage your Agile information flow well. The more you know about your release plans the greater the advantage you have. The less you know about them then the lower the chance you have of success.

Sun Tzu Said: *Probe the opposing force for its strengths and weaknesses. Then look at your own strengths and weaknesses and compare the two.*

Gauge your Agile team's strengths and weaknesses against the task at hand.

The balance of victory for your Agile team is not an absolute but it is a relative measure. What works in one situation may not work in another; there is no one solution that fits all. Great Agile teams mold themselves to the current situation and create their agility based on their circumstances.

Linda, the Scrum Master for Team Ultra, had the team co-located for the first few months in the UK and they were working face to face. Linda had built great rapport in the daily standup and the product owner really liked meeting the team this way. But the next year the team move to an offshore site and Linda had to adjust to making the Agile team work in a non-collocated way. Linda had to reach in to her toolkit and make Agile work in this new setup. She used WebEx and Video Conferencing to help bridge that gap.

Sun Tzu Said: *Everyone can see results and how the battle was won but none can see the strategy out of which victory is evolved.*

Some successful Agile team's are like ducks that look calm and collected as they float majestically on a lake. But if you were to look underneath the surface you would see their little legs paddling furiously to keep them moving.

Being a successful Agile team takes hard work and dedication to bring out the passion and deliver great software. It is important to remember that after all the hard work the most important thing is the outcome - did your team deliver that great bit of software on time? Getting that right is what Agile is all about – it's not just about delivering fast but minimizing the work done and getting to see those great results.

Sun Tzu said: *Do not reuse the same tactics which have won one victory, but instead look to varying them accordingly.*

Your Agile team cannot expect to always use the same skills or strategy through life because the world is always changing. Your team are better off if they keep moving and going onto bigger and better things. Always look to stretch the team to help them grow and become more than they were yesterday.

Sun Tzu said: *Strategic tactics are like water, which runs from high places to low places. Avoid what is strong; you should strike at what is weak.*

Ensure that your Agile team takes the path of least resistance as they remain focused on their goal, not on various problems they encounter along the way. Deal with those problems effectively and move on. The great Agile team is all about doing less and getting more.

Sun Tzu said: *Just as water is in no constant shape, so in warfare there are no constant conditions. Modify your tactics in relation to your enemy.*

By getting your team to focusing on the sprint goal and looking for solutions your team can find ways to reach their goal given the resources that they have. Sometimes the solution is sitting in front of them, but if they don't place their awareness in that direction, they won't see it as the way forward.

Get the Agile team to remain aware that the conditions

in which they work are constantly changing and adapt their tactics accordingly. Ensure that they keep learning and upgrading their skills to meet the needs of the marketplace.

Sun Tzu said: *The five elements (water, fire, wood, metal, earth) are not found in equal measure; like the changing seasons each one will have its turn to be predominant. There are hot days and cold days and the moon has it cycles.*

All team members have a different set of personal attributes. While some team members are quiet and diligent, others are outspoken and insightful.

We all, however, have been given the gift of self-determination. We can choose to make the most of what we have and work towards being successful in whatever we do.

A great cross functional team is not one where all team members are clones of the other members, but rather their individual energies merge collectively to form into something that is greater than the sum of their parts.

VII. Maneuvering

Sun Tzu said: *The general at war receives his commands from the sovereign.*

Your team's beliefs and passions power their feelings, which lead them to take actions toward success.

- People are very important and know how to do their job better than those managing them
- Completed software is a better indication of where you are than whether you are working towards your plan
- Quick feedback between customer and developer is essential

Sun Tzu said: *If you look to equip you soldiers with full gear and set to march to obtain an advantage then you may be too late, having wasted much time in getting ready. However if you are swift and send out a light response unit then you may get an advantage but at the expense of providing little food and provisions for the response team.*

Preparation does not require perfection. Act as soon as you are ready. Great Agile teams do not wait for the requirement to be perfect as they seldom are. What is really important is our ability to respond to change. Agile team should feel 80% confident with the user stories and they are able to estimate the size so that it is sprintable. To offset the fact that requirements are not always 100%, the product owner or business analyst should be readily accessible to provide clarity when required during all key touch points.

It is important to have access to the business analyst or product owner during the standup, review and during the day.

Sun Tzu said: *Even if you have loyal men who march on orders at double speed to cover more ground, covering a large distance in a short time to help secure you an advantage, you may find that ultimately they will be captured by the enemy as fatigue sets in.*

While a journey of a thousand miles begins with a single step, it is also a marathon and not a sprint. Pace yourself and your team for the long haul so you can maintain the strength you need to reach your goal - keep a sustainable pace to your delivery. Use your intelligence and planning so you can finish and have that victory. Don't set your team up to fail due to mental, physical, or financial exhaustion.

Plan your software delivery so you have enough resources to finish the race.

An important metric to keep track off is the amount of

motivation that your team has. Are they feeling de-motivated today or really fired up?

You can keep track of this using the Niko-Niko Calendar, where you write each day of the sprint on the board and take a reading from each team member. You can print some emoji out and paste them to magnets which can then be stuck on the board for each team member. This is a great way to track the team motivation. You can also ask the team what kind of things that can do as retro action, which will help them become more motivated during the sprint. You might find that they want to spend some time reading about a new JavaScript library.

Sun Tzu said: *Place your best men in front and let weary souls trail behind and this plan will deliver just 10 percent of your forces to the chosen destination.*

March 50 miles to outflank the enemy and you may find your leader might die of exhaustion and only 50 percent of your forces reach their target.

March 30 miles to reach the same target then 66 percent of your forces will arrive intact.

By trying too hard to reach your goals you may find that your efforts will be counter-productive.

The probability of success is reduced if you try too hard with too few resources or you try to push too hard for too long. There is an art to reacting to a situation and applying the right pace so you get things done as quickly as possible but without suffering burnout.

Jason, the Scrum Master of team Toxic, has 5 developers and 1 tester for his Agile team. Jason has to deliver over 10 user stories every sprint for the next six months. Every sprint that went by was a nightmare for Jason, as his developers produced code and got stories implemented only to find 5 stories were started, but were still in progress at the end of the sprint, 2 other stories were completed and the final 3 were in testing.

Every sprint that went by Jason's team became more and more frustrated by the fact that they couldn't complete all of the stories that keep piling up and spilling over.

Jason should have spoken to his boss and asked for more resources, which would have helped the team get through the work. It is clear to see that if Jason had at least 2 more testers then he would have had more of his stories completed.

Agile is not about doing the impossible from sprint to sprint – it's about having as little waste as possible.

which means having the right resources to ensure things get delivered.

Sun Tzu said: *If you move your armed forces without supply wagons then all is lost; if you have no food and water then all is lost; without a base to resupply your forces all is lost.*

Your Agile team may arrive at their destination victorious, but at what cost?

Winning at any cost is not always ideal. What's most important is to achieve success through planning, strategy, and maneuvering so you still have your team intact from the point of their physical health, their mental health, and your project's financial health at the end and can enjoy your victory.

Sun Tzu said: *Don't enter in alliances until you know others' agendas.*

Entering into alliances with other Scrum teams, whose skills vary from your own can be very advantageous and can result in outcomes that are much more successful than you could otherwise hope for. It's essential that you approach this correctly, as any one hoping to scale up agile to delivering it at enterprise level will need to deal with this. Take, for example, those wanting to use LeSS or SaFE and they will encounter these issues when they do planning for say 5 Scrum teams. It is important to have an enterprise Scrum Master who is neutral to all the 5 teams so that the planning session does not become stacked in favor of the 'Lead' Scrum Master of one particular team.

What often happens is team A's Scrum Master might be working as a team scrum master for his own team and also leading the other 4 Scrum Masters in the planning meeting. Team A's Scrum Master may be inclined to push all the difficult tasks to the other teams so that all the easy low hanging fruit goes to his team.

This may not be the best thing for the overall delivery of the project because team A may deliver all their work at the expense of team B, C, D, E which may fail to delivery their work due to incorrect allocation of user stories. It is better for the business to hire a neutral enterprise Scrum Master who does not have a team, but looks out for the welfare of team A, B, C, D and E. This enterprise Scrum Master can ensure that the work load and user stories are balanced in the best possible way for all the team to deliver successfully. This enterprise scrum master can also look to handle issues and blockers for all teams in a neutral way.

Take time to find out as much as you can about the other potential Scrum teams. Consider their motives and how they will benefit from working with you, as well as how you can protect your team from becoming unbalanced when you work with other Scrum teams.

Sun Tzu said: *Do not enter territories unless you know its dangers and the tricks and traps that await you.*

Learn as much as you can about the organization when

you are helping them adopt Agile for the first time. You should spend time getting to know how things get done in the organization. Who are the people that are allies in your quest to get Agile into the workplace? Who are neutral? Finally, who are the objectors and will impede the adoption of Agile transformation?

Sun Tzu said: *When in a foreign land you should look to leverage the knowledge of local guides if you wish to take advantage of the local terrain.*

Seek out the help of guides when entering new territories. Learn from the expertise of others. As a Scrum Master helping the organization get going in Agile, you should start to build a list of Agile supporters and build a community where these like minded people can meet and drive that change across all of their respective areas.

Tony is the Scrum Master and Agile Coach for a leading financial institution and he sets to work getting to know all the various people in his department. He got talking to the Test Lead and the Head of the BA team. Tony suggests that they form a group, which would meet up on a weekly basis to discuss how they were going to drive Agile change across the department and, going forward, how they were to bring this to the wide arena in the other departments.

Sun Tzu said: *The decision to concentrate or divide forces must be based on the situation at hand.*

Observe the organization around you and be proactive by taking advantage of opportunities as they arise from changing circumstances. When you find that your Agile transformation is growing and the initial team that was setup is no longer meeting the demands of the business, then it becomes time to think about dividing the team in two so that you can grow and spread the Agile team to support the need demands.

It is important to split a team in a way that allows fresh members to join a team who know Agile well rather than try to duplicate the one single great Agile team. If the second team is built from all new members it will have difficulty catching up with a mature Agile team that has been working for 2 years or more. It's always best practice to seed a team with 2 members from the old team and all new blood in from there.

Sun Tzu said: *Be as swift as the morning wind, and as impenetrable as the forest trees. When attacking and raiding move like a forest fire and when on defense be like a rocky mountain.*

Your Agile team should move quickly when

opportunities present themselves or when danger arises, but don't take unnecessary risks. Having all the issues and opportunities on a big visual board will help your team stay focused on the software delivery aspect rather than just the development part of the project.

Sun Tzu said: *When you loot the enemy be sure to divide the spoils among your soldiers and when you have gained new lands be sure to share out fairly to your men.*

Keep the gears of Agile success moving smoothly by rewarding everyone involved in each of your victories. Create as many win-win scenarios as possible. Don't just leave all the juicy stories to your top developer, always look to share fairly so that the bug fixing BAU can be shared across each developer rather than it being given to one person. By rotating the different tasks at hand, your team will appreciate that they can all share in doing interesting things and keep motivation high.

Sun Tzu said: *Think and consider before you take action.*

As a Scrum master you should consider your resources and all other variables, such as issues and timing, before you take your first step. Often it is great to build a release plan and vision document with the product owner to help crystallize and clarify the approach and SoW. Getting a technical architect in to help create a high level design document will be useful to provide a framework around which the teams can work. Building the technical runway is important if you want the team to succeed and is even more important when you have multiple teams working on the release.

Hardy, the Scrum Master for team Helios, spent the first few weeks working with the product owner to help shape the vision document and build that critical release plan, which gave the project shape. Before they could do some high level estimate it was clear that an architect was needed who could look at the existing system and provide the overall building blocks for what a solution could look like and the required technology stack.

Sun Tzu said: *Learn the artifice of deviation. That is the art of maneuvering.*

Continuously enhance maneuverability and resources by building up Agile Knowledge, paying down technical debt, cultivating relationships, and ensuring the team are learning new skills.

VIII. Variation in Tactics

Sun Tzu said: *When you enter a difficult country, do not rest and bed in. When you are on high ground shared by others look to create alliances with them. Avoid dangerous isolated positions. When you are hemmed in, use strategy. When all else fails and you are in a desperate position then and only then you must fight.*

Do not rest on the assumptions that agile strategies for success that have worked in the past will continue to work despite the rapidly changing face of the economy.

Many businesses are finding that the waterfall way of doing things is not working anymore and the demand for agility is constantly increasing. It is critical that Agility is not just about developing good software but also about getting it to market quickly and ensuring that it's the right software at the right time.

Use a multi-faceted approach through which you apply agile tactics and ensure that they are unique to your situation and applied dynamically as needed. If you find that your team is finding the sprints are holding the team back for becoming more Agile, then look to see if you want to move to a Kanban approach to deliver features as and when needed. This may be more useful when the platform is stabilized and the project is now in BAU mode.

Remain very fluid and open to take advantage of

opportunities as they arise - think about adding different agile elements as and when needed.

When you feel hemmed in, strategize a way out - ask your Agile team to look toward tactical solutions to meet the needs at hand. And when all else fails, meet the situation head on and use all the resources you've gathered along the way to land on your feet - even adding additional resources as needed, for example in sprint 2 and 3 you may look to align additional developers and testers from another team. You might also want to align a specialist from the other team such as the BPM, SSIS expert for a sprint or two.

Sun Tzu said: *There are some roads you must not travel and some enemies you must not engage, there are cities you must not besiege and positions you must not contest. And there are commands that must not be followed.*

Just because you can, doesn't mean you should. Every child who tastes a favorite treat for the first time wants more. They want to eat it instead of dinner and eat it seven days a week. But most children are limited from indulging constantly in their favorite treats because such actions will lead them to become sick and unhealthy.

As a Scrum Master, always help your team to be Agile,

rather than just doing Agile by helping them think before they act rather than working from impulse to satisfy each and every one of their Agile desires. Team's should use method and discipline to keep themselves healthy. Daily standup and retrospectives are key to keeping teams in shape, otherwise a great Agile team can start to stray from the path and revert back to old habits.

Sun Tzu said: *The general who is well versed with a variety of tactics will be able to take advantage of a given situation and use the resources and men at his disposal.*

Learn to balance your Agile team's actions against the results your team are trying to achieve. Budget your resources and time, for example, so your team can spend less time on rework and more on doing work that adds value to the project. Some days your team will need to do a lot of pair programming and other days they just need to work solo to get their heads down and focus on the task at hand.

Sun Tzu said: *A leader may know his country well but if he does not understand these tactics he will not be able to execute his plan effectively.*

Scrum Masters should give all of the team members training in Agile and especially with regards to the Scrum framework. Knowing the framework does not make the team an expert in Agile. The team needs to really understand the mindset behind the Agile practices so that they are being Agile, which is a mindset change rather than just doing Agile, which is to follow a set of steps without the passion and understanding attached to it.

knowing the framework is one thing, but sticking to it is another thing which takes time to master.

A Scrum Master needs to help team members understand why they must do something so that they can have the conviction they need to carry out the task that is required.

If you can, help developers and product owners understand that spending time re-factoring will help ensure that the software is maintainable over a period of time, which will save the business money in the long run. Doing this will make it easier for people to give room to developers to re-factor their code within the sprint.

Only once you understand such reasoning can you take steps to create the necessary bandwidth to ensure good technical engineering practices are followed, such as re-factoring, TDD, design patterns and peer code review.

Sun Tzu said: *A student of war who is not well versed in how to vary his tactics and plan will fail to make full use of his resources and men, even though he may know of the five advantages.*

You may understand the five basic elements of the scrum values:

(1) Focus

(2) Courage

(3) Openness

(4) Commitment

(5) Respect

But without coaching your team and the organization on the values of these so that they can embrace them then the cause may be lost. Agility can only flourish when the environment allows it to. Like a farmer who plants seeds for the harvest, without water and sunlight the seeds cannot hope to grow until these are present, in the same way that Agility cannot be adopted unless there are fertile minds that love these Scrum Values.

Don't be like a billboard, stiff and inflexible, snapping in half when enough force is applied. Be like a branch on a tree that is supple and survives even the strongest of winds because it's flexible and bends as needed - that is the true nature of a great Agile organization.

Sun Tzu said: *A wise general will look at the pros and cons and blend them to form a workable plan.*

Part of your Agile release planning must include an assessment of the pros and cons of each of the user stories in the product backlog. Why are they there? What value will they add to the delivery? Where should they be in the ordered product backlog list. This will help ensure that your release plan forms a workable plan.

Again story mapping with pro's and con's can help in deciding what really matters for the delivery. The product owner or business analyst should be able to stack the user stories in a way that tells the story of the delivery.

Sun Tzu said: *Even if not all the variables are to our liking we may still have a workable plan that we can use to reach our target.*

When building our release plan we might find that there are a number of dependencies, which may not be to our liking. We are never going to have a perfect plan, so we need to be flexible when looking at the dependencies. We might have to have parallel tracks of work going on to compensate for these dependencies. We might have to break the release into two releases.

For example, Scott the Scrum Master for team Tungsten was working on Release 5.0 and his team was dependant on a component being developed by another team in the business, which was running late. Scott talked to the other team's Scrum Master to ask him to break their release into two parts, so that he could delivery one in time for the first part of his backlog which was critical. Then a second release was created by both teams to handle the rest of the backlog, which was then delivered 2 month's later.

Sun Tzu said: *When we are faced with difficulties we can still win if we put to good use the advantages and opportunities do present themselves.*

When life gives you lemons, make lemonade.

A great Agile team should look to maintain a positive attitude when challenges arise so that they can remain open to any opportunities that may arise as a result.

Richard, the Scrum Master for Team Iodine, was struggling for desk space in his office, which was not very Agile. He had asked the floor manager and HR for 1 desk per team member. He was told he would have to wait for 6 months for his request to be looked into. Instead of cursing his luck, Richard was able to find an office that was being vacated and put the whole team in there with a big desk. This was a great place for the Agile team to bond by sitting very close together and working on laptops rather than the clunky desktops.

This small office on the floor created a really great Agile environment as the team were able to decorate the office with all their metrics and charts. They also were able to talk freely and have the product owner drop in for chats with the developers and testers. This would not have been possible had Richard got his original wish of 6 desks for his team.

Sarah, the Scrum Master for Team Klax, was not able to find a space to do a stand up where the team was located. She also wanted to have a couple of whiteboards where the team could put this scrum board and project tracking details. Having spoken to the floor manager, she located an empty cove near the print hub which was not being use and was able to put 3 whiteboards in there and made that the war room for her team.

Sun Tzu said: *In the art of war we must not expect that the enemy will not come but we must prepare ourselves for his arrival by making our position unassailable.*

An Agile team cannot expect the product backlog to be perfect. Instead they should welcome change; a changing world creates opportunities. Be prepared and ready to grab hold of change and let it help drive a better product forward to delivery. The point of Agile is to learn something about the product after each and every sprint and change user stories in a way that maximizes the newly discovered knowledge. Scope does not creep but understanding grows. To make your position unassailable, carefully manage your resources and let the product owner know that, yes scope creeps or new knowledge should be embraced but they need to know that the team has only a finite no of stories point for the release and to add new change they need to drop out less important items from the current release backlog. The product owner will need to prioritize the changes they want vs. what is already in the product backlog and be prepared to drop items out.

Roxxane, the Scrum Master for Team Helium, was in a meeting with the product owner, Tom and they were discussing the sprint review. Tom was pleased with the work done so far, but could now see that he would need a new story created to handle PayPal payments for his shopping card, which was not currently in the product backlog. Roxxane suggested that they could analyze and estimate the new user story and, given its size, Tom could prioritize it against his current product backlog with one caveat, which was to keep the total number of stories point for the release in the 500 point limit. In this way Team Helium was able to respond to and accept change, but also keep the delivery on track by keeping the release to 500 points. Tom understood this and dropped the 13 point story for Market Information Reporting in favor of a 13 point story for taking PayPal payment.

Sun Tzu said: *A leader can be affected by any one of five dangerous faults:*

(1) Recklessness, which often leads to destruction;

(2) cowardice, which can lead to being captured;

(3) a hasty temperament, which can be easily provoked;

(4) a thin skin, which is highly sensitive to shame;

(5) sentimentality, which exposes him to feelings of worry and endless troubles.

These five sins can be the ruin of a great general and can occur once he is at war.

(1) Being reckless can lead to one's own demise. Before using a new Agile practice the team should think first and act later, rather than trying to recover from a bad situation, because they couldn't be bothered to think it through before you entered it. Guard against being reckless. Agile is about learning and trying out new things, but it should be tempered in a way that will provide for control exposure in the same way that chemists have controlled environments.

(2) Being a coward can lead to one's own demise. Rather than an Agile team making excuses and procrastinating and then missing out on opportunities when they come along, they should take action and seize the day.

(3) A hasty temper or lack of emotional control can lead to one's own demise. A Scrum Master should ensure that meetings and discussions with the product owner and development team are not a pitched battle, but rather a focused set of objectives being confirmed.

(4) Being thin-skinned can lead one to be overly sensitive to challenges or insults and act recklessly as a result.

A Scrum Master should coach the team on these matters and act as a barrier to ensure that insults and reckless behaviors do not arise.

(5) Being too worried about those around you can cause you to make mistakes.

As a great Scrum Master you should look to coach your Agile team in the five scrum values, so that they are able to focus and do what is right.

Sun Tzu said: *When the general is killed and the army has been crushed the reason will be found in one of the five dangerous sins. Let us make these findings a matter of inquiry for our minds.*

Master the five scrum values so you can avoid these

pitfalls.

IX. The Army on the March

Sun Tzu said: *When we are looking to bed in and create a base camp we should look first to see any sign of the enemy. We should travel over mountains as quickly as possible and stay close to green valleys.*

When you are looking to setup Agile in an organization, it is important to make sure that the team members are 100% on the scrum team and not share across a number of project and teams. Only dedicated Scrum Team members can delivery great results, otherwise a resource will be overstretched if shared over a number of projects and teams.

Sun Tzu said: *Take the high ground and the well lit location.*

The high ground provides a strategic advantage. Achieving high ground can be as simple as moving the Agile team to areas that the team can call their own, instead of just the open-plan office. This could be a section off-area, which gives the team the feeling of security and self identity.

Sun Tzu said: *Take care of your resources and men and build your base camp on hard ground. This will ensure that your men are free from diseases of all kinds and will ensure you have the best chance for victory.*

Disease may come in many forms: physical disease, mental disease, social disease, or even software disease.

Physical disease can be caused by working in a stressful environment. Agile environment can be stressful with the continuous expectation of delivery at the end of each sprint. To help prevent that, one should ensure that the team does not commit to more than they can handle and always build in some spare time to allow the team to work on their retrospective actions.

Mental disease can arise if your team members suffer from discrimination or intimidation at work, which can lead to mental disease. As a Scrum Master you should ensure that all members are treated fairly and have an equal say in all matters. Post-It notes help to alleviate that problem.

Social disease can strike when your team members are surrounded by negative office colleagues, especially those who discourage them from taking steps toward positive change in their work life. A Scrum Master should always look to ensure that the environment is positive and healthy. NLP and reframing can be useful tools for the Scrum Master in these matter.

Software disease can occur when your team are beginning to suffer from technical debt. For example, they need to add a drop down list to the UI screen and wire up the back end, which now takes 5 days worth of work. This is because of the layers of architecture of old code which the team have to look through, for example 10,000 lines of asp code. The code base was not maintained and new lines were added all the time until the asp page was 10,000 lines long.

Clearly in this case you have got a software disease that has put you into a lot of technical debt. It is better to refactor code along the way rather than at the end of 5 years' worth of work.

Sun Tzu said: *When you are on a hill or a bank keep on the sunny side with the slope at your back. This will provide you with a good tactical position.*

Your Agile team should utilize the natural advantage of the ground. If you put in months' of effort to get TDD put into place within the code base, then take advantage of the many opportunities that come with that. The team can look to go with continuous integration and also ask the business analyst or product owner to put the acceptance criteria in BDD Gherkin Syntax.

Sun Tzu said: *If it has been raining and the river you wish to cross is swollen wait until the water subsides.*

When your Agile team is working on user stories in the product backlog, it is useful to work on items that are closer to the top of the product backlog and not spend too much time analyzing later product backlog items. These late product backlog items are still in flux and as such they may be subject to a lot of changes.

Sun Tzu said: *Terrain that has steep dangerous cliffs, hollows and confined places with branches and thickets should be left immediately or avoided altogether.*

Your Agile team should put checks into place to prevent missteps from happening, for example your sprint team should have an internal playback within the sprint for the implemented user story. Doing this internal playback helps to ensure that the product owner sees the work as soon as it is ready to be shown, rather than waiting for the sprint review.

Stories that are too large for one sprint should be broken down into smaller easily digestible stories.

Difficult and risky stories should be broken down and measured against the risk and reward model to ensure that we are truly getting value for money.

Sun Tzu said: *If you send men to gather water and they sit and rest and drink before returning then your armed forces are suffering from thirst.*

It is important to put systems in place to track your resources and get alerts when trouble arises. A burntout team is no good to anyone so your team should always keep fresh by maintain a sustainable pace.

- Build activities into everyday work - do not leave testing to the end of the sprint, but have them spread out. Test Analysis, Test Design and Test Execution should be done as soon as it makes sense to do it.

- Keep iteration to short durations, such as 2 weeks and playback often.

- Question long hours and provide fruit to the team as a part of the business cost.

- Try to limit the repetitive work by using design patterns.

- Ensure planning is done in advance so that the team is not stressed and ensure that grooming happens often enough to make user stories sprint ready, instead of doing the requirements during the sprint.

When running a sprint keep watching the visual scrum board to see when work is not flowing and highlight blocker with the stop magnet. Address any blockers quickly to keep the team moving smoothly. Make use of RAG status on the board if you want to monitor the health of the user story and ask the team what they can do to restore the health of that story.

Sun Tzu said: *If the enemy has found an advantage but does not make a move to secure it then you may conclude that his forces are weak and suffering from exhaustion.*

When your Agile Team has seen an opportunity but does not seize it right away, then consider the possibility that they are suffering from exhaustion.

If your Agile Team feels constantly stressed and suffers

from the feeling of being disillusioned or helplessness then they may be suffering from exhaustion.

Get your Agile team to take steps to regain their balance by first looking at their priorities and making time for rest and recuperation. If your Agile team are too tired to do this then seek support from those around you. As a Scrum Master you should speak to your line manager or the development manager to enquire as to what options are available. There could be a number of options such as moving the team to a quieter part of the office or providing days out for training or social activities.

Some causes of stress are related to feeling that they have little or no control over their work or their work environment, or feeling that their efforts are not appreciated. As a Scrum Master you should look to providing ample opportunity for team members to vary their activities, as well as placing trust in them doing a good job. At the end of the sprint a Scrum Master can run the appreciation retrospective to help provide a stage for all members to thank someone in the team.

If your Agile team are not inspired or challenged by the work at hand, they may be discouraged by its monotony and dread facing it each day. As a Scrum Master you should look to encourage them to learn new technologies and meeting people in the community of practice. Also, brown bag sessions can be good for those who like to talk about their favorite subject matter and are excited to share their latest finding.

The quick checklist below might help you see where your team members may be having issues:

- Are they feeling tired and drained on a daily basis?
- Do they suffer from frequent back pain, or muscle aches or spasms?
- Do they feel they have lost their appetite and find it difficult to sleep well?
- Does your Agile team suffer from minor ailments and catch colds easily?
- Does your Agile team feel a sense of failure or have feelings of self-doubt in retrospectives?
- Does your Agile team feel defeated, trapped, or have a sense of helplessness?
- Does your Agile team lack motivation?
- Does your Agile team have a negative outlook at work and feel very cynical about the project?
- Does your Agile team find themselves avoiding

responsibilities?

- Does your Agile team find themselves avoiding interaction with the stakeholders and often keep to themselves?
- Does your Agile team find themselves procrastinating and making excuses and putting things off?
- Do you find any team members lashing out at other people and later feeling guilty about it?
- Do you find any team member coming in late to work and leaving early?

If you can tick off more than 50 percent of these then your Agile team may be suffering from exhaustion and/or depression.

Remedies that you may want to consider:

As a Scrum Master take time to talk to each team member to find out if there are any issues or troubles which are causing them to feel burnt out and demotivated. Find out if there are any people who are causing them issues or any process that they are finding it hard to adjust to.

Ask if they would like to spend more time pair

programming and who they think would be a good mentor if they should need one.

Get in to a healthy routine. See if management can bring a fruit basket that provides the energy they need throughout the day. See if management can put in a vending machine with good snacks or if smoothies can be delivered to the office.

See if the business/HR can provide a discount to a gym membership. Look to have a few retrospectives in the pub or in the park with some snacks and sandwiches. Look to organize a lottery syndicate for the team so that everyone feels a sense of camaraderie.

Help your team to prioritize their task list, so they do what's most important first and other matters are scheduled for later.

Don't give false expectations by promising that your Agile team will do the impossible. This will only lead them to have a lack of faith in their ability to cope with the demands.

Get the Agile team to pace themselves, so they can meet their commitments.

When it's sunny outside take time to let the Agile team go for a walk.

Sometimes sharing is one of the best ways to get the Agile team on the road to recovery. Run a retrospective that focuses on the difficulties that the team are currently facing and how they might meet those challenges.

Consider the bigger picture and see if your Agile team has moved in a direction in which there is now a mismatch between them and their software environment. You might want to reassess the Agile team's goals and priorities.

Ask your Agile team these questions:

- Are we happy with the current Agile process?
- Are we getting enough contact with the product owner?
- Are we using the best technology and equipment?
- Does the office environment provide the best Agile space in which the Agile team can work?
- Does the Agile team understand and feel passionate about Agile?

These are some basic questions that can help your team reassess their goals and priorities and lead them to take steps toward positive change in their work life.

Sun Tzu said: *A general who takes his opponent lightly and does little thinking before attacking will surely be captured.*

As a Scrum Master, avoid making assumptions about anyone or any situation. Work from facts alone.

Focus on asking the right questions that help you solve a problem or understand a situation.

Don't fill in missing information by making assumptions based on preconceived notions. Agile is all about learning from empirical evidence rather than assumptions.

Ask questions until you've gathered all the relevant facts that allow you to make an informed judgment.

Don't assume a product owner who hasn't responded to your email doesn't want to speak to you. Call him and ask about it. You might find that his computer was down and he couldn't read any of his emails.

An Agile team operating on assumptions can lead to wasted time and resources, stress caused by misunderstandings and miscommunication about co-worker or product owner needs and lost business opportunities.

Your Agile team might lose a client if they fail to provide what he needs because they have assumed what he wants is what is best for the product. What the product owner wants may not always be what they really need and reviews are great talking places to find out what they need rather than just what they want.

Don't let your Agile team underestimate their product backlog. Let them communicate and gather the facts so that they can fully understand what's going on and take the most effective action. Don't let the Agile team make assumptions.

Sun Tzu said: *Soldiers must be treated well but trained through the regular enforcement of orders so following them becomes a habit. This will make your men disciplined.*

The adoption of Agile practices requires a certain level of discipline and routine. Progress can be difficult to achieve if one day you do what you are supposed to do and the next you do something completely different.

Your Agile team should work on their Agile practices each and every day so that it can become part of their routine. Over a number of sprint retrospectives, you should be able to review this and see how they are progressing.

For your team to make a habit stick they need to make it part of their daily routine for an extended period of time. Some people say it takes at least two months to form a habit; others say it takes at least three months. What's most important is that the habit is practiced every day so that the brain's neural connections can be rewired so one does something automatically.

It's also true that you can change behavior with greater focus. So if you focus on become more efficient and collaborative you will become more efficient and collaborative. After spending 90 days focusing on looking at ways to reduce waste, your team will find themselves attuning their minds to the benefits of doing so and it will lead them to think of more ways they can reduce effort rather than expend their efforts.

Agile team's should strive to be disciplined so they can bring—and keep—successful habits into their life.

X. Terrain

Sun Tzu said: *Insubordination occurs when the men are of strong will but their leader is of weak will.*

A Scrum Master should be a leader who demonstrates the value of Agile in their working life. A good Scrum Master uses a Kanban board to track their issues and retrospective actions. A great Scrum Master should be at each and every daily stand up. A great Scrum Master should be passionate about Agile and always look to find better ways to improve themselves and their team.

Progression is an important key to success. You need to grow as a person and help those in your team increase their confidence.

In life there are no shortcuts. You need to spend time and effort building your skills and those of your team.

A great Scrum Master and servant leader values his team's opinion and regularly seeks them out. If your team does not provide a diversity of opinions then they are not in a servant-lead organization.

A great Scrum Master and servant leader cultivates trust within his Agile team. He/she does not need to micro manage his staff, but lets them reach their full potential by working to their passions.

A great Scrum Master and servant leader helps foster this trait so that his team take responsibility for their time at work.

A great Scrum Master and servant leader cares about his team's progress in work and in self development. A great Agile team is one that celebrates not just their work victories but also birthdays, weddings and retirement. A great Scrum Master should always help the team celebrate all great things worth celebrating in life.

A great Scrum Master and servant leader encourage his team by leading them through difficulties with a 'let's do it' mantra rather than a 'you go get this done' mantra.

A great Scrum Master and servant leader is a great sales person who uses the gentle art of persuasion to motivate and lead his team forward rather than others who use the old command and control way.

A great Scrum Master and servant leader is always thinking about what is best for the team rather than themselves. All actions and thought should be directed to what needs to be done so that the Agile team and their members can be as effective and safe as possible.

A great Scrum Master and servant leader is also thinking about tomorrow as well as today because tomorrow's problems will become today's problems. A great Scrum Master will consider what can be done today to pay down technical debt so tomorrow we don't have to worry about it.

A great Scrum Master and servant leader will act with humility so that the Agile team can focus on the most important tasks. Developers write software, testers make sure it is tested and has no defects and Scrum Master does everything else to ensure that all things run smoothly. This could be as simple as booking meeting rooms, arranging passes for people to get into the office and bringing post-it notes and pens to the meeting. A great Scrum Master maximizes the time that a developer and tester has available to do their tasks. At the end of the day Agile software delivery is about having some software written and tested and if they are too busy filling in paper work and doing too much admin then who is going to write the code and test it?

Sun Tzu said: *Collapse will occur when the officers are of strong will but the foot soldiers are of weak will.*

A great Scrum Master and servant leader is only a brick in the wall. Without a great Agile team software delivery wont happen.

A great Scrum Master should look to turn those un disciplined scrum members into a well oiled machine. Often, a well oiled team of average scrum members can beat a unorganized group of hot shots.

Sun Tzu said: *When senior men are upset and angry they* *will show insubordination and fight the enemy on their own without waiting for their general to issue orders. This will bring about ruin to the army.*

Diving into an Agile transformation without the support from senior management will not deliver the result that you were expecting. It is critical that you get the support from the relevant heads so that the Agile transformation programme has the best possible chance of success. This should be done through presenting the benefit of Agile in the language that best suits your audience. For head of development it might be, how will this streamline the development process and ensure that delivery is on time. For the business it might be, how the Agile transformation programme will enable better use of resources and the ability to absorb change.

At project level this will translate into the programme team needing to have the right resources and skills hired for the project and a vision document prepared.

Sun Tzu said: *If the general is of weak will and lacks authority, if his orders are not clear and he has not given a structure for his senior officers to follow then the ranks will be formed in a messy manner. The result of such a situation is total and utter disorganization.*

For an Agile transformation programme to be successful the sponsor for the programme should provide a clear vision of what they are trying to achieve and in what time frame. There should be milestones and a clear indication of what good Agile looks like. When people know how success will be defined in the Agile world then all people under them can work towards that goal. If the goal is 'let's be more Agile', then the transformation programme will not be as successful as it could be.

For an Agile project the programme manager should clearly define the goals and plan related tasks accordingly, so they can be executed in an organized manner and lead to your success. The best way to do this is to create a visual Agile roadmap on the wall so that all stakeholders can collaborate and discuss the roadmap. If you are not co-located then a spreadsheet with the date and a WebEx will be the next best thing.

Sun Tzu said: *When the general is unable to gauge the enemy's strength, thus allowing a weak force to engage a stronger one, or allows his best men to be placed at the rear, the result is a rout.*

When looking to deliver success in an Agile transformation programme one should look to bring the brightest and most passionate people to the programme. When an initial programme is started, any negative or disruptive people can derail those early starts. You will need to bring those people onboard, but only when the programme has made some gains that can be used as evidence to show the green shoots of progress.

For an Agile project you should look to assemble a team of bright and passionate people who really want to do great Agile. If the team is not keen then either they need to be coached early on or removed from that team so as not to disrupt the Agile project.

Sun Tzu said: *A wise general who can go forward and attack without looking for fame, retreat without fearing shame, and who's only thought is of the welfare of his countrymen is a true hero.*

Your ego can be your undoing, so strive to tackle projects and tasks objectively to avoid the distractions your ego might otherwise create for you.

A great Scrum master and servant leader thinks about the welfare of his Agile team and does not look for fame for himself but for the betterment of his team. If one approach is not working there is no shame in adapting and moving on, because what's more important is failing fast or, in other words, learning quickly from early attempts and moving on.

Sun Tzu said: *If you know yourself and know the enemy, then victory need not be in question; however if you know the nature of the ground you are about to conquer, then ultimate victory will be in your own hands.*

When looking to roll out Agile in a transformation programme, it is important to know what level people are within the organization and what coaching and practices will deliver maximum impact for the programme.

Kieran is an Agile Coach and having spoken to the business he found that the real pain point for them was the drag and waste created in trying to create good user stories. This was the key area that Kieran identified as being what should be targeted first and foremost. Kieran knew that the business analyst and PMO needed to be coached in working in a much more agile way and he spent the next few months defining what good looks like and how the business analyst were to get from their current position to what good looks like.

Your Agile transformation programme success depends on the ability to get them operating like well-oiled machines. You need to keep all the parts moving smoothly, including gathering requirements and creating user stories, to developing and testing and deploying this to production. Value stream mapping can be invaluable when you are looking to see what can be made more efficient. You might also run a number of retrospectives and do root cause analysis.

XI. The Nine Situations

Sun Tzu said: *The art of war identifies nine types of ground:*

(1) dispersive ground

(2) facile ground

(3) contentious ground

(4) open ground

(5) ground of intersecting highways

(6) serious ground

(7) difficult ground

(8) hemmed-in ground

(9) desperate ground

Sun Tzu said: *When a general is engaged in battle on his home ground, that is called dispersive ground.*

When looking to adopt Agile in the business, you should first adopt Agile in your current team and work location. What can be done to transform your current office to make it more Agile? Can you be creative with putting up big Scrum boards which could be the use of an old wall or window. You don't need to order in a fancy digital board which would take time and cost. You can look to build your product backlog in Excel if you don't have

JIRA or Rally. In fact it's better to have your Agile Artifacts in a physical format so that people are drawn into your Agile space. It is also important to get your stakeholder into your Agile space for the daily stand up rather than using a WeEx where possible.

Sun Tzu said: *When a general has penetrated into hostile ground but by only a short distance then that is known as facile ground.*

When looking to start an Agile transformation programme, you should investigate all areas of the business and where there is most promise for the adoption to begin. Who are the strongest advocates for the Agile transformation programme?

Do your preliminary research before you commit any resources, knowing you can back out easily early on.

For an Agile project you should explore an number of Agile tools before committing to anyone of them. When building your Agile board don't grid it straight away as you will be making it rigid. Instead, look to keep it open by using whiteboard markers so that you can chop and change columns and swim lanes as your team becomes more mature.

Sun Tzu said: *The ground that if secured would provide great advantage to either side is known as contentious ground, which is contested for.*

When you are looking to help the organization adopt Agile, there will be those who would like waterfall to stay. In these situations it is important to look to start Agile in an area where there are new projects and there is the appetite to move quickly without having the old waterfall mind set getting in the way.

For an Agile team, it is important to get all members on the same side, wanting to work and co-operate in an Agile way. One way to achieve this is to have a big Scrum Board that the team can get around, which will help everyone adopt the Agile mindset. Doing a stand up without a whiteboard or not near it or having a small one is going to lessen the ability to create that Agile mindset.

Sun Tzu said: *When the ground has ease of movement for both parties then that is known as open ground.*

This is ground in which all players small and big can work and no one has a clear advantage. This is where great collaboration happens because everyone can speak freely, which creates the transparency that is required to make Agile work and remove blockers.

A great Scrum master should look to create this environment where all parties can share and collaborate without fear of reprisals.

Agile teams will move faster when they are able to adapt and continuously improve without fear of failure. We should all look to build a culture of continuous learning and improvement.

Dan, the Agile coach, is always working toward creating that environment where people can collaborate without fear of failure. Fail fast, Fail often is not the best way to express the culture of Agile, despite how catchy it may sound – what we really should talk about is Learn Fast, Learn Often.

It's about learning rather than failing and Agile success comes from an environment that can foster and embrace the culture of learning. We should cultivate an Agile environment where all parties can inspect and adapt. This drives lean methodology of 'Think big, act small, fail fast, learn quickly'.

Sun Tzu said: *When three lands are joined, the person who occupies the land that intersects the other two has the command of the region.*

A great Scrum Master and servant leader should sit in the land that intersects the other two – business and technology.

By being in the middle, a great Scrum Master is able to see both sides of the coin and provide neutral ground in which the Agile environment and culture can flourish. A great Scrum Master does more than coach and enforce the scrum framework. They are the life blood in which agile software delivery gets done. An organization without a great Scrum Master is likely to suffer from waste and blockages.

Sun Tzu said: *When a general has moved his forces into the heart of hostile territory such that he is surrounded in all directions by fortified cities he has entered into serious ground.*

When Agile transformation has reached wide and far in the organization, then it is important to have support from all the CIOs because a lot of energy and resources have been expended to get there. As a programme, the full commitment should continue, so rather than being driven for 6 months, the programme should have enough backing to reach multiyear investments which will allow the business to fully reap all the benefits that come from being fully committed and all those involved should be prepared to compete and win.

Sun Tzu said: *When the terrain gives to chasms, bogs, and marshes, land that is hard to travel then this is known as difficult ground.*

Difficult ground can be likened to an environment that has a lot of people who are either disruptive or skeptics.

Fear of the unknown is one of the reasons why people are skeptical. As a great Scrum Master, you can address this by providing scrum training and coaching. Asking them to attend the daily stand up can be a tonic to help with skeptical people.

Disruptive people need to be shown the light, that the transition to Agile is happening because it is what the organization needs in order to stay competitive in the market place. By them not being committed to proceeding with the transition, they are effectively putting themselves out of a job by not helping their business staying competitive and successful.

A great Scrum Master should show them that in fact the Agile transformation is actually a great opportunity to grow the business and make it more future-proof, and without their help the competiveness cannot be maintained and therefore job security and promotion cannot come about. A great Scrum Master can let them know the disruptive ones can help and make the difference between success and failure of the organization and they can play a great role in making things better.

Sun Tzu said: *When the path narrows and you find yourself surrounded by chasms and gorges and your sky is that of solid granite; and if a small number of soldiers were to find you there then they would crush you even if you were a larger force, then that is hemmed-in ground.*

Hemmed-in ground is often encountered when your business is in a contracting market in which less and less money is flowing, but commitments such as office leases, homes, cars, and equipment remain. An Agile transition success is critical in ensuring that the business gets pulled out of hemmed-in ground. When developers, testers and anyone on the Agile transformation path sees these they will realize that everyone should think Agile and look at what can be done to become more productive with the resources they have on hand.

On an Agile project, hemmed-in ground can be when there is a tight deadline and not enough people to complete the user stories in the product backlog. A great Scrum Master will look at all options with the programme team to brain storm the way out using the retrospective meeting as a key transformer for moving forward.

Sun Tzu said: *When you have entered into grounds where the last resort is to fight at all cost then you have entered into desperate ground.*

Desperate ground can provide a fantastic opportunity for Agile transformation because it clears the way for change. An Agile coach doesn't have to fight with skeptics or disruptive people because everyone is motivated to make it work.

For an Agile project and team the desperate ground is a time for thinking creatively - what are the kinds of things we can do that can help us become more efficient? Desperate ground is fertile soil for providing that catalyst for which change can happen.

Peter is the Scrum Master for Team Radox, which has an offshore and onshore set of members. They were behind in their sprint and Peter was desperate for a way to get the user stories completed that week. He was able to schedule the team offshore to work IST time in India and then check in and hand over the work to the UK so that then could carry on in GMT time. This extended the 'working day' from 8 hours to 15 hours. Peter's team was able to complete the sprint on time due to this creative thinking.

Sun Tzu said: *When you are on contentious ground you should not attack. When you are on facile ground do not stop but keep on moving; and when on dispersive ground do not fight.*

Do not rest on facile ground because there you are exposed. When beginning an Agile transformation programme you should look to keep the momentum up on the adoption of Agile. Dont stop before you have reach the full potential which only come in after you have pass facile ground. Dedicated and passionate Agile transformation programmes keep improving year in, year out like business, such as Apple and Google. It is not a destination that is reached but a state that should be maintained.

When working to deliver software at the project level, the great Scrum master should keep prompting the team to follow and continue with the Agile practices. Only when they know it by heart can they move on the next level. Think of Shu Ha Ri, which comes from the Japanese martial arts Akido. Shu is the beginning stage where the student follows the teaching of one master precisely. Ha is where the student branches out. Ri is when the student is now learning from his own practice. Don't let the Agile team's progress stop at Shu, but keep going to Ha and then finally the Ri stage.

Avoid wasting your energy on contentious ground. Instead use all your energy and resources to build your Agile transformation up as quickly as possible, so you can gain an advantage in locations that welcome and embrace Agile change.

Agile teams should avoid wasting their energy on contentious ground. Instead, they should look to gain advantage by working with those who welcome and embrace Agile change.

Sun Tzu said: *When you have entered open ground then you should not try to block the enemy's movement. If you find yourself on ground that borders another force then look to create an alliance with them.*

Do not try to block the enemy when on open ground as it does not provide any strategic advantage. When helping a business with their Agile transformation you should welcome all those on open ground and let their ideas come to the table to be shared and worked on.

For Agile teams, the great Scrum Master should not block someone from making a suggestion, but let everyone have their say but time box it for those that like the sound of their own voice!

Sun Tzu said: *A general who finds himself on hemmed-in ground should look to apply his stratagem, but when on desperate ground time is of the essence and he must fight.*

Through the process of adopting Agile, the organization my find itself hemmed-in. In these situations they need to apply stratagem and find tactical solutions to overcome challenges. A lot of organizations are hemmed-in, due to not having the full funding to do the Agile transformation across the whole organization so a tactical solution could be to apply Agile adoption precisely in an area of the organization that is facing severe challenges.

For Agile teams that are finding themselves hemmed-in, in these situations they should look to find tactical solution through brain storming in the retrospective.

When time is of the essence in an Agile transformation programme, the efforts should be place in finding quick win solutions which delivery maximum effect. Agile training and coaching always pack a good punch and can be rolled out quick in less than 6 months across the large parts of the organization.

When time is of the essence in an Agile project, the efforts should be placed in ways to de-scope what is not needed. It is quicker to drop work that is not needed than to try to find ways to ramp up the team velocities. MoSCoW analysis can help in these matters.

Sun Tzu said: *When a general finds an advantage he should move forward to capture it; but when an advantage does not exist he should stop and wait until like a hawk he saw an opportunity to strike.*

When you are involved in the Agile transformation programme, it's important to know when to take the process further. When there is support from upper management this is a great time to look to push through new initiatives.

A great Scrum Master will help the Agile team take advantage of new opportunities that arise though coaching and put actions into gear.

Sun Tzu said: *Swiftness is the key essence of war and you should look to take advantage of your enemy's inattentiveness and travel by unconventional paths that enable you to launch attacks on his unmanned positions.*

Agile coaches can push the Agile transformation through by inviting all interested parties to an Agile Drop-In Session, where regular informal discussion occurs. Questions can be answered and experiences can be shared. In this way everyone is welcome to join in and push the Agile transformation forward by learning about it in the drop-in session rather than be pushed to learn it as a directive.

Sun Tzu said: *A general who is invading his opponent should know that the further he moves into hostile territory the stronger his men's morale will become as they build on their early victories.*

The further you progress in your Agile transformation programme the more momentum your advocate will carry. As your programme builds this momentum, you should be able to advance to higher and higher levels of Agility, for example, setting up a community of practices will be straight forward. This is the point at which momentum starts to take over from your hard work. Initially a boulder hardly moves, despite the great force you exert. But once you push that boulder over the top and to the downward sloping part of the hill then gravity takes over and all your hard work pays off. The most important thing to remember is to not block the natural momentum, but instead provide conduits for it to follow. It becomes a matter of steering the Agile transformation rather than pushing it along.

A great Scrum Master at project level should be building on the team's early victories by creating more and more lofty goals for them to achieve.

Sun Tzu said: *When on the move your army should look to gather food and water and supplies from the surrounding area. They may need to spend time doing this, putting the main campaign on hold while they replenish their resources.*

For an Agile transformation programme the Agile Coach should be looking to keep the pipeline filled all the time by looking for new value streams, new advocates, and other valuable opportunities. Often it is good to take stock of where you are in the programme and present the findings and take readings through meetings and retrospective workshops. Showcase current progress to all interested parties.

For an Agile project it is important that the Scrum Master takes the time to set retrospectives up, which will allow the team the chance to digest what they have learnt and pivot from that new vantage point. Great Agile teams do not move in a straight line, but are pivoting from one vantage point to the next; learning as they go from point to point.

Sun Tzu said: *A good general should always monitor the well-being of his soldiers and should not overwork them. He should always look at ways to boost their energy and strength while keeping them on the move. He should also keep such a maintenance plan impenetrable and unknown.*

A great Scrum Master should establish a regular maintenance plan to keep all of the team's skills and knowledge in top condition.

It is more cost effective to keep all your resources and assets well maintained than let them fall into decay and then have to spend a vast amount of time, energy, and money restoring them.

Sun Tzu said: *If you put your men into situations where there is no retreat then they will surely fight will all their might as death is their only other option. When faced with death your men will surely choose to live.*

When men have been placed in a dire position all their sense of fear is removed and they stand their ground and fight like ten tigers.

A great Scrum Master understands that by putting something at stake you will increase your chances of success due to the increased motivation. If you put nothing in, then you have nothing to lose and thus are not committed.

This is why it is critical that the Scrum Master gets the team to choose a sprint goal for themselves.

This is why it is critical that the Scrum Master gets the team to choose a name for themselves.

This is why it is critical that the Scrum Master gets the team to choose their own definition of done.

This is why it is critical that the Scrum Master gets the team to build their own scrum board.

This commitment to doing things as a team creates that camaraderie that is so critical to the great Agile team.

Sun Tzu said: *Do not let your men discuss omens and consider superstitious piffle. Then they will fight will the heart of a tiger and fear nothing until death takes them.*

A clear mind is essential to being successful. A clear mind is free of negative energies that cloud understanding and lead to critical mistakes. A clear and healthy mind means that bad luck will be kept to a minimum and opportunities will be maximized.

When looking to adopt Agile through an Agile transformation programme, it is essential to have everyone work from a clear mind, free of negative energies. 'Good luck' is when preparation meets perspiration, and passion is often the secret ingredient to making this Agile transformation programme successful. The same can be said for a Scrum Master operating at the project level.

Sun Tzu said: *When the day arrives and the men find that the orders to begin battle has come, you will find some may shed a tear or two as they say goodbye to their loved ones but once they have looked into their souls and seen their destiny and seen the vision of their general then each man will have no less than the courage of ten tigers.*

Passion greatly increases the chances of victory. Money is just a way of keeping score; there must be a deeper force propelling you to success. If you are able to tap into that passion you will find that your victories will be many and sweet.

Passion can also reveal courage, which might surprise you and those around you.

For an Agile transformation to be successful, passion is definitely the key to making it work and this means getting to know what makes people tick. What are the things that really matter to the people in the organization? When we are able to answer these questions then great progress can be made.

For some it is about avoiding waste.

For some it is about building the better product.

For some it is about customer satisfaction.

For some it is about working with respect.

For some it is about working with integrity.

For some it is about providing a better service.

For some it is about striving for excellence.

For some it is about great stewardship.

Find these touch points which people care about at the programme, project and team level - taking action will go a long way to making your Agile transformation work smoothly.

Sun Tzu said: *A skilled military general may use the form of* *a shuai-juan which is a snake found in the Chang Mountains. When you strike this snake on its head it will fight back using its tail. If you try to strike its tail then you will find it bites with it head. However this snake if you try to take it by the middle it will strike with both ends, biting you with its head and whipping out at you with its tail.*

Is it possible that this form is found in that of men? If two armies were to cross a river in the same boat that was hit by a storm and water was to come onto the boat all the men would take to buckets to move the water as soon as could be possible.

As the human body is formed with unity, the left side helping to balance and work with the right side, so that is what you must consider in the art of war.

If your Agile team plays only on the offensive then they will always leave themselves exposed by not looking after their defensive positions.

If your Agile team plays only on the defensive then they will always leave themselves exposed by not looking after their offensive positions.

When your Agile team masters both defensive and offensive play, this will then ensure ultimate victory.

Sun Tzu said: *A general should not just chain the horses to the tree and remove the chariot wheels and bury them. One must do more if they are to inspire the men to battle like ten tigers. Their passion must be found and brought on the field of battle.*

It is not enough for your Agile team to be intelligent and knowledgeable about their area of expertise. They must have passion, drive, and purpose in order to maximize their chances of victory.

Sun Tzu said: *A general is given what he has, he cannot change that; some of his men are strong and others are weak– he should not try to look to see if he can be dealt a new set of cards or bemoan his lot; he should consider how best to use his men on the battleground that he finds himself on. Like water to the vase he too should find his men as fluid and flexible to their terrain.*

An Agile Team should know when to use their strengths and also when to use their weaknesses.

An Agile team should use their strengths in the most critical of positions and then use their weakness when success matters least.

When the Agile project is going well, for example, your team can work on developing their less well-defined skills. This might be them refining their test driven approach or their design patterns or paying down some technical debt.

When the Agile project is not going so well then they should focus on their core competencies. So this might mean they need to limit the work in progress and focus on getting user stories completed without trying to gold-plate everything.

Sun Tzu said: *A skilled general will manage and lead his army as easily as if he was giving personal instructions and orders to a single man.*

A great Scrum Master should be able to handle the small things such as making sure that all tasks are updated on the scrum board as well as making sure that the whole project gets delivered.

A great Scrum Master should understand how to look at things from the ground up so when you delegate you can quickly know if others are doing a good job.

Sun Tzu said: *A great general must consider the different measures and how they would be applied to the nine types of ground; he should think whether to take the offensive or defensive approach and he should consider human nature and how it will react in such matters. These are a matter of personal inquiry and in the night before dawn should be contemplated.*

The nine varieties of ground must be studied but to be truly a master of them you need to think out of the box rather than consider them as fixed rules.

Learn to apply Agile with the nine varieties of ground, but be flexible and adaptable so you can apply them fluidly in any given situation. The ability to be flexible and adaptable can be key to your survival.

Sun Tzu said: *When a general has pushed himself and his men deep into hostile lands, the nature of man is that they are brought closer like a brotherhood of men. However if they have only gone but a short way then they may be easily dispersed like pigeons.*

Once you have made a commitment to adopting Agile then the only way to see it through is by committing yourself whole heartedly to it and then you must follow it through to the end.

XII. The Attack by Fire

Sun Tzu said: *When you are looking to attack your enemy you should first check to see if you have the means to complete the task.*

In order to launch an Agile project you need to have your resources ready.

Look to hire people who have the right skills, which make them great cross functional scrum players. It is also important to hire people who have the openness to try new things and have a can-do approach. Even if you hire one person who is not open to Agile this can derail a good team, so be on guard because it is very important to have 'can do' Agile people. Skills can be picked up but people with the Agile mindset are worth their weight in gold.

Sun Tzu said: *When you are looking to use fire as a weapon you should check to see if the conditions favor such an attack. What season are you in? Is the weather warm and dry; are the leaves and grasses parched with the lack of rain from the past three moons?*

Timing is very important in making Agile work in an organization and team. You should check to see what level of fluency the organization is at and also what level the various teams are at. Once you are armed with this knowledge it will be easier to introduce Agile to people at just the right level.

Sun Tzu said: *Does the wind blow in the same direction as that of your men; these are the days that you must consider. Then the time to start a fire is here but take care to not begin if you have the winds blowing to you or if there is a feeling in the air that the winds may change.*

It is better to take action in the direction in which the wind is blowing.

When you move along the path of the wind you have the forces of nature working with you; in this way you follow the path of least resistance.

The same is true when looking to adopt Agile – seek to find where the wind is blowing and follow the path of least resistance.

For Agile teams you should consider the practices that they have in place and how they can be adapted at each iteration to improve their agility. People are more happy when they are in transition rather than using a rapid shock approach. A great Scrum Master should get to know the team and where they are in their Agile maturity and take things from there.

Sun Tzu said: *A wind that comes in the early morning will carry throughout the day but the breeze that comes at night can end as quickly as the rain may end on an autumn night.*

It is important to get the Agile practices established as quickly as possible because the Agile team will keep them as a good set of habits from the start. Once a team picks up a bad habit it may be difficult to set a new precedent.

Sun Tzu said: *When a general wins his battles but does not find rhyme or reason to his orders from his sovereign his spirit and that of his men will wane and unhappiness and stagnation will follow.*

An Agile Coach or Scrum Master can only do so much for the business but without the full support from higher management then the adoption of Agile will start to suffer. Hiring a Scrum Master and not supporting them in the adoption is going to make the adoption process very difficult. It is important that higher management sends out clear signals that the whole business is looking to shift. The Scrum Master is going to facilitate this on a day to day basis, but they need to know that he will be supportive throughout the transition.

Sun Tzu said: *The wise and enlightened sovereign will have a vision and this he must share with his general if he is to inspire his general and his men.*

A CIO who is looking to adopt Agile at team level and at programme level must share his strong vision with his management team. The Scrum Master or Agile Coach must not be kept in the dark if they are expected to succeed. Often the CIO would expect the Agile Coach to do everything possible to make Agile work, but it is also true that the CIO is respected at board level and should clear the way for this transition to occur.

Sun Tzu said: *A wise general will take no action unless he can see a tactical advantage; he will keep his men on standby unless he will gain something; he will only issue orders to attack when placed in a position of desperation.*

Do not change Agile practices for the sake of it to show change. What is more important is to look and inspect what is happening and only then adapt and take just even action to make the system work again. That is the heart of being Agile and lean. The secret is in the frequency of the feedback loop to enable that change to occur. Inspect often and adapt when needed.

Sun Tzu said: *A wise general would not put his men to battle for his own glory or be tempted to engage when provoked.*

Agile Teams should look to evolve at a pace which is right for them, rather than run before they can walk. Stretching the team is important, but straining the Agile team should be avoided unless you want to have a burnt out team.

Sun Tzu said: *A wise ruler knows that anger can change to gladness, like a caterpillar into a butterfly. Unrest can become contentment given time; so a wise ruler should know that an empire once destroyed cannot be rebuilt. The dead cannot rise and be brought back to life. So the wise ruler should always be mindful and keep his empire at peace and his army cohesive but on standby.*

When a team starts on the path to adopting Agile they will be new to the process and perhaps even resist that change. Therefore, it is important to let the process unfold so that the team can get into the continuous improvement mindset rather than be force-fed Agile until they take it or break because of it.

XIII. The Use of Spies

Sun Tzu said: *To raise an army of 1,000,000 men and move them across 1,000 miles would surely drain any great nation of its resources. The daily cost of keeping such an army on the move and well fed would surely cost a thousand ounces of silver. There will be commotion at home and abroad and many men will fall by the wayside. Yet foreknowledge enables the wise sovereign and good general to strike and conquer and achieve things beyond the reach of ordinary men.*

Your Agile team will benefit from knowing what is happening in the world and the marketplace. Knowing the marketplace is critical to ensuring that the team make informed choices and take appropriate actions.

Sun Tzu said: *Foreknowledge cannot be gained by talking to the spirits or by reasoning with one's experience or other method of deduction. It can only be found by talking and gathering from other men.*

Knowledge can only be gained by going out and looking for it. Ensure that your team has time to look at and learn about new technologies so that they can keep up to date.

The closer you are to the source of knowledge, the more reliable it is. Ensure that the Agile team receives training when new technologies come out so that they can put these into practice as and when it becomes useful.

Sun Tzu said: *To ensure proper management of them you should be open and sincere and keep good will with them.*

When you let your Agile team go out to meet-ups and other organizations, to see what works well for Agile you should look to take on any advice they bring back. Listening to them will ensure that their time has been well spent, as most of these events are in the evening and are in the personal time of the people in the teams.

Sun Tzu said: *Without subtle cleverness, one will not be able to make certain of the truth of their reports.*

Information gathered by your Agile team from meet-ups should be viewed objectively in case it is inaccurate. Other organizations may have oversold their Agile method or approach. Validate whatever information comes your way and strive to understand where it was generated and how it was acquired.

Sun Tzu said: *Be discreet and use your spies whenever a situation presents itself.*

Success depends on a constant information flow. Acquiring vital information should always be a goal, but so should the protection of your own information. You should not talk about sensitive project information at these meetings as this may cause problems for your organization with regulations etc.

Sun Tzu said: *The converted spy is the most important because he will know the enemy best. It is essential that he be treated with the most tolerance and good will. Without the converted spy you cannot make use of the surviving spy.*

Recruit experts in the field of Agile and your programme will go well. Always look to hire great talent that can help drive that change forward. Learning from those who have implemented Agile before will enable your transition to begin smoothly.

Sun Tzu said: *A great leader will use the highest intelligence of the army for purposes of spying and thereby achieve great results. Spies are the most important element; on them depends an army's ability to move.*

When you hire a Scrum Master and Agile Coach who have been at other places, they will have a wealth of knowledge that can help provide you with lessons learnt from many other implementations of Agile. Look after your Agile Coaches and Scrum Masters and you will be Agile.

Michael M. K. Cheung

XIV. Conclusion

Sun Tzu's wisdom has helped me remember that Agile is not just a list of practices and meetings it is something that you live by - you should live the wisdom of Sun Tzu's ideas and practice them each day. Sun Tzu has also taught me the benefits of remaining flexible and always striving to grow and to be more Agile each and every day.

Most importantly, I have learned that Agile is about being proactive and excelling in everything you do whether it is work, rest, or play.

I hope you too will be able to apply the wisdom of Sun Tzu, so you too will live long and prosper and have a full and rewarding life, as well as deliver great software.

Sun Tzu and The Art of Agile Software Delivery

Contact Information

Twitter:

http://twitter.com/agilesuntzu

Email:

michael.cheung@agilesuntzu.com

Website:

http://www.agilesuntzu.com

www.ingramcontent.com/pod-product-compliance
Lightning Source LLC
Chambersburg PA
CBHW071421050326
40689CB00010B/1934

* 9 7 8 1 5 3 0 3 3 5 7 2 5 *